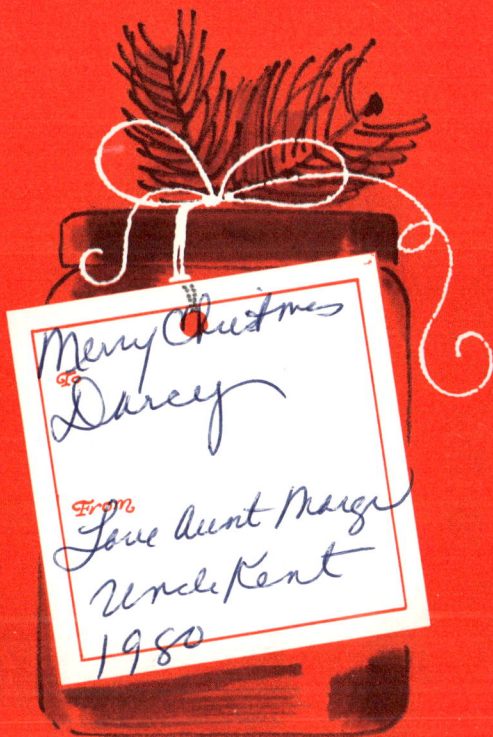

Merry Christmas
To
Darcy

From
Love aunt Marge
Uncle Kent
1980

A
Gift
from the Kitchen

By Audrey Romoser McGaffin

Designed and Illustrated by
Roland Rodegast

Published by The C. R. Gibson Company, Norwalk, Connecticut

To my husband and family who cheer-
fully ate the monsters from recipes that
are not included here, to Len Kaufman,
one of the Other People, who talked me
into writing this book, and to all the
known and unknown originators of
many of the trophies captured herein.

Contents

OTHER PEOPLE

Three weeks ahead,
Their shopping's done;
Their gifts are wrapped.
We've not begun.

Two weeks ahead,
Their cards are gotten,
Stamped and mailed.
Ours aren't boughten.

One week to go;
With proper pride
They trim their tree.
Ours lies outside.

On Christmas Eve
A virtuous quiet
Pervades their house.
We have a riot.

A GIFT FROM THE KITCHEN
IS A GIFT FROM THE HEART

What This Book Is All About . . .

Are you one of the Other People mentioned in the foregoing? Then you might as well put this book down. If, on the other hand, you are the type of lost soul who winds up at the last minute buying assorted linsey-woolsey staples for gifts; whose mind congeals when faced with the multitude of tasks; who watches sadly as your recipients' faces fall upon opening those un-inspired, often wrong-sized horrors — then, dear kin-dred spirit, this book is for you. I will take you step by painless step to a Christmas where you will be a star giver of gifts finished and wrapped so far ahead that you will have time even to re-read good old Scrooge's tale and watch Amahl and the Night Visitors on tele-vision. Read on.

List of recipes

COOKIE TROPHIES

Chapter I

Before the Hoorah Starts Part I

What to Buy . . . What to Do

Acquiring Christmas gifts in Spring goes against the grain as much as splurging on garden tools in November.

Don't fight it, for you can kill two chores with one pot shot by preserving goodies both for your table and your Christmas gift list. You won't object to closet shelves bulging with the trophies of your advance planning when you know the booty will vanish on Christmas Day accompanied by your recipients' hoop-de-doo of joy.

And remember, on your first time out you don't have to bring down *all* the trophies pointed out to you by your guide. A few garnered each season will improve your skill while loading your gift bag gradually but surely.

Now, for those hunters whose Mommas never done told 'em, the following first steps will eliminate frustration and tears.

STEP 1

Have basic ammunition on hand. You can acquire the following at either your community department or five-and-dime stores:

Two large (6 to 8 quart) cook pots
Several packages cheesecloth
Small-mouth jelly funnel
Wide-mouth funnel (for preserves, relishes, etc.)
Long-handled cooking spoon
Grater
Large bowls (3 and 4 quart sizes)
Round colander
Dipper with pouring lip
Measuring cup with pouring lip (for liquids)
Measuring cup with no rim above 1-cup line (for solids)
Set of measuring spoons
Pair of tongs (size used to handle corn-on-cob)
Pressure sensitive labels, or a roll of freezer tape.

A word of explanation about some of the above items is in order here. Two large cooking pots are better than one because you will usually need one for sterilizing jars and/or glasses while you are cooking the trophy's ingredients in the other.

You'll need cheesecloth for either a large bag of four thicknesses of the cloth or for at least one and a half yards folded into a four-thickness square to place over a colander set in a large bowl, to separate juice from fruit for jelly. Always dampen the cheesecloth before using to prevent waste of juice.

If you won't be satisfied with anything but the clearest jelly you must use the cheesecloth *bag,* hanging it up with the cooked fruit in it for several hours or overnight to let the juice drip out, *never squeezing;* in using this method, you'll find you will have to use one-half again as much fruit for the amount of juice obtained because a part of the juice will remain in the pulp. However, now that I inform you that although squeezing may result in a bit of clouding of the jelly, but does not affect the taste or keeping quality, you may decide to save time and fruit by using the square of quadruple-thick dampened cheesecloth.

Place the dampened square of cloth over your colander and set the colander firmly in a large bowl. Pour or ladle the fruit into the center of the cloth. Allow to cool, then twist the ends together and press the cloth with a masher or alternately squeeze and twist the cloth to extract all the juice. Be careful not to squeeze so tightly that pulp or seeds will be pressed through the cloth into the juice.

After discarding the pulp, seeds, etc., the cheesecloth may be washed in warm water and then placed in a bowl of bleach solution to remove any fruit stains. Rinse thoroughly to remove the bleach, then dry thoroughly before storing. Throw away the cheesecloth square or bag when the threads begin to separate, leaving small holes through which seeds or pulp may slip.

Many trophies call for the addition of grated lemon or orange peel. When using a grater, you will find it much easier to place the grater on a large sheet of waxed paper instead of resting the bottom of the grater in a bowl; the grater tends to slip about in the bowl, endangering your knuckles.

Use tongs to remove glasses or jars from boiling water, and to place lids on jars.

Wipe any spills from rims with clean paper towel dipped in boiling water.

Hold each jar with oven mitt or clean tea towel and screw bands on tightly.

Pressure-sensitive labels are better than the old-type glue-coated ones which have a tendency to come loose from jar or glass after a time, leaving you with a passel of assorted unknown quantities. If you cannot locate these labels in your community, you may make attractive labels from freezer tape, by cutting it into two-inch lengths and trimming the edges with pinking shears.

Be sure to label each batch of goodies before storing. Since some trophies are similar in color it is surprising how easily one may be mistaken for another if unlabeled.

It is a good idea to keep a large sheet of paper and a pencil in your gift closet, perhaps hanging on the inside of the door. As you stow away each trophy bagged, jot down the number of jars and its name. If you give away or use any trophy, be sure to deduct the amount from the total number of jars as soon as you remove it from the shelf. This record will be invaluable when you begin your gift-allotting in December.

An ounce of forethought is worth a pound of hindsight so in deciding which trophies to hunt, you should try to take into consideration the needs or preferences of your recipients.

For example, for a relative or friend who has young children, you may want to give her mostly the simple fruit jellies, so good combined with peanut butter as a sandwich filling for school lunch boxes and also good as a topping for cottage cheese or cooked cereal. For those people on your list who are allergic to a particular fruit or vegetable, you will undoubtedly decide to hunt trophies minus such troublesome items. For the housewife on your list who is a fellow-huntsman of note, you will want to bring down a few extra-special unique trophies, and for the friend who lives in another section of the country, you may choose trophies containing a special fruit or vegetable from your region.

Of course, if you are fortunate in having a list of people who have no preferences or problems and who love to eat just anything good, you have it made!

After deciding to hunt a particular trophy, check the number of jars it will fill. Then count the lucky names on your list who will receive a jar of this trophy and add the number of jars you will need for home use. You will now know whether one batch will cover your total or whether you will want to double the trophy recipe. It is better, when bringing down trophies containing liquid or powder fruit pectin such as Certo or Sure-Jell, to make two *separate* batches since you must have room in your cook pot to bring such trophies to a full rolling boil. Double batches of the long-simmering type can usually be made in one pot since they cook slowly enough not to boil over.

STEP 2

This list of ammunition can be acquired at your grocery store or supermart:

> Half-pint (8 ounce) jars with lids and bands
> Jelly glasses (8 ounce size)
> Paraffin
> Bottled fruit pectin, such as Certo
> Powdered fruit pectin, such as Sure-Jell
> Ingredients called for in chosen trophy.

Half-pint jars are best for gift-giving of preserves, relishes, con-serves and chutneys. They hold just enough to whet the appetites of your friends and relatives so they will look forward to the next Christmas each year. Also, if you have many names on your list you can give a greater variety of trophies to each person since half-pints go around farther than larger jars.

For jellies, the eight-ounce glasses are best for the same reasons. If you are fortunate enough to have a young baby in the family, rescue the discarded baby-food jars. Any friend with a baby will be happy to save hers for you if you promise to put her name on your gift list! These jars are just the right size for gift jellies and jams, for six varieties in little jars are better than only two in large glasses.

While on the subject of saving, stash away the plastic trays in which tomatoes, mushrooms, etc. are packaged at the supermart. These trays will hold three or four baby-food jars of goodies.

12

When you get to the stage of having something to wrap, I'll tell you how to fix the trays and wrap them for safe delivery on Christmas.

Another good item to save is the larger instant-coffee jar, the kind that holds six ounces of coffee powder but will hold almost a quart of homemade mincemeat. Oh yes, I will guide you to the lair of that paragon of good taste, the mincemeat trophy, a bit later in the year.

If your jelly glasses come packaged in styrofoam-type trays, one dozen to a tray, save the trays. They are easily divided into two six-packs with a knife, and each six-glass tray will eliminate the problem of finding a large suitable container for your gift of six jars.

Canning jars and jelly glasses (or baby-food jars) *must* be sterilized before using. First wash and rinse the jars, then cover with boiling water in second large cook pot. Add funnel and dipper, and boil at least five minutes to sterilize. When the jelly or preserve mixture is just about ready, remove jars from hot water, using tongs, and invert on a tray covered with paper towels to drain. *Glasses or jars must be hot* or they will crack when the mixture is poured in.

When using canning jars with lids and bands, it is necessary to submerge the lids in boiling water for a few minutes just before sealing the jars. It isn't necessary to sterilize the bands, but be sure to wash them before using. A shallow pan such as a layer cake pan makes a handy utensil because each lid may be placed in the pan without putting one lid on top of another, and heated in a minimum of water quickly. If one lid slips into another when using a smaller pan, the two resist separation mightily.

When using jelly glasses or baby-food jars, you *must seal* the contents with paraffin. This is best melted in a clean tin can which can be discarded afterward, saving a messy clean-up job. Press the top edges of the can together slightly to make it easier to pour out the paraffin without spilling. A folded paper towel held just under the pouring edge of the can will prevent stray drops from running down the side of the can or of the glass being filled.

Set the tin in a pan of hot water and place over a low flame to melt. Two thin coats of paraffin are better than one thick one. Pour in about $1/8$ inch for the first coat; when it becomes opaque and hard, add another small amount of paraffin, tipping each glass slightly and rolling the wax around the edges of the first coat. This ensures a good seal.

Most of the baby-food jars now on the market have screw-type caps that contain small rubber seals. Do not depend on these seals for air-tight protection once the jars have been washed and sterilized; always use the added protection of paraffin. When filling these jars with jelly or jam, be sure the mixture comes up to the neck of the jars, in order to prevent paraffin from getting under the "bend" of the neck. If paraffin does get under the "bend" it is difficult to remove when opening the jelly for use.

If you have bagged a trophy in canning jars, don't jump into your gift closet when your cooling jars sound as though they are shooting at you! Each lid will make a popping or clicking sound when the cooling jar becomes vacuum-sealed. Greet each pop with joy for it tells you that *that* jar has been sealed properly. If you lose count of the pops, tap each lid with a spoon when the jars have thoroughly cooled — they should each make a ringing sound, and each lid also should be depressed slightly. If, alas, any lid fails these tests, better open and reheat contents to boiling, then reseal with a fresh lid.

Chutneys, preserves, marmalades and conserves are thick mixtures which tend to acquire air bubbles when ladled into jars. These bubbles not only spoil the appearance of the finished trophy, but may cause spoilage of the contents in time. So check your jars as you fill them and remove any air bubbles by slipping a sterilized spoon handle down, into the mixture, to the bubbles to liberate them. Sterilize the spoon handle by dipping into boiling water for a minute or so, or drop a spoon into the pot with the sterilizing jars, dipper and funnel. NEVER touch the contents of a jar with unsterilized utensils. NEVER allow filled jars to stand unsealed for more than the time it takes to put on the lids and bands. The air in even a spotless kitchen carries the threat of spoilage to trophies that are allowed to stand open for more than a few minutes.

One last admonition for the beginning hunter. Read over the list of ingredients in the contemplated recipe the day before hunting and buy any ammunition you don't have on hand. Don't be like a forgetful friend of mine who bags her trophies in the wee small hours while her husband moonlights on his second job. She arrives at my house, wild-eyed, at 3 a.m. demanding a lemon or a cup of sugar because she hadn't checked her supplies before drawing a bead on her quarry.

Reread this chapter just before beginning each hunting trip, to refresh your memory so you can find some particular paragraph more readily in case you want to recheck it as you progress.

Gun-shy? Lost your nerve already? Relax. After the first time out, all will become familiar and you'll be a Dead-eye Dick at hitting each target without reading the manual more than twice. You will barely remember that I was once your guide. Such is fame.

Chapter II

Spring at A Small Quarry

Starting with Strawberries

Made up your mind to be a good sportsman? Good! Now it's Spring, time to make like a big-game hunter. Concentrate on one trophy at a time and just follow your guide to success.

Hike to the Supermart Woods to bring home a brace of boxed strawberries plus the other necessary ingredients for Trophy #1. On your return, sing a round of Jingle Bells (it does evoke the proper mood especially if accompanied by a bit of left-over Christmas cheer) and lay out your ammunition to capture this delicious quarry.

It makes an impressive topping for ice cream or other desserts, being whole plump pieces of fruit in clear red syrup. It should be a welcome Christmas trophy.

16

1. PRESERVED WHOLE STRAWBERRIES

2 quarts firm ripe berries
5 cups sugar
1/4 teaspoon salt

2 tablespoons light corn
syrup
1/4 cup lemon juice

Rinse berries, drain, remove caps and measure. Put berries in a wide shallow bowl and add rest of ingredients. Gently mix with hands until all berries are coated. Let stand 5 or 6 hours.

Cook over low heat till sugar dissolves. While berries are heating, sterilize 8 8-ounce jars, wide-mouth funnel and dipper.

When the sugar on the berries has dissolved, turn up heat and bring to a boil. Boil rapidly for 15 to 18 minutes or until berries look "clear" and the syrup thickens slightly.

During the last few minutes of cooking, sterilize 8 canning lids, and remove jars from hot water and invert to drain.

Skim off foam from berries during the last minute of cooking. Fill the hot jars. Remove lids from hot water and place on jars; add bands and screw on tightly. Place jars on side to cool. If berries rise in syrup, leave jars on side for 3 or 4 days, turning a bit each day. Then label and store.

• For the gourmet on your list, the following prize can't be topped. Take advantage of the strawberry season while it lasts and make this easy piquant trophy.

2. STRAWBERRY-SAUTERNE PRESERVES

4 cups (about 1 quart) small
ripe strawberries
4 1/2 cups (2 lbs.) sugar

1 box Sure-Jell fruit pectin
1/4 cup sauterne wine
1/2 cup water

Measure 4 cups (firmly packed without crushing) strawberries. (If berries are large, halve them.) Layer berries and sugar in a large saucepan. Add wine. Let stand at room temperature 4 to 5 hours, mixing once after about 2 hours. Mix carefully to avoid breaking berries.

17

Before heating fruit mixture, sterilize 6 8-ounce jelly glasses, wide-mouth funnel and dipper. Melt 1 bar paraffin.

Then place the fruit mixture over medium heat, bring to a full rolling boil and *boil hard 2 minutes,* stirring constantly. Remove from heat. Mix Sure-Jell and water; bring to a boil and *boil hard 1 minute,* stirring constantly. Mix into hot fruit. Skim off foam. Stir and skim mixture 8 to 10 minutes to cool slightly and prevent floating fruit. Remove glasses and invert to drain. Fill drained hot glasses. Cover with hot paraffin. Cool, label and store.

• Another delightfully tart trophy, as exhilarating to the taste as Spring is to the sight, is this combination jelly. If you own a blender you will find it a wonderful time-saver and labor-saver in preparing the juice — and the fruits need no preliminary simmering, either!

3. STRAWBERRY-RHUBARB JELLY

1½ lbs. rhubarb
  1 quart strawberries,
    fully ripe

5 cups (2¼ lbs.) sugar
1 box Sure-Jell fruit pectin

Trim off leaves, cut off root ends, wash rhubarb and cut into 1-inch pieces. Do not peel. Wash and cap strawberries. If using blender, blend fruit at slow speed, one cup mixed fruit at a time, till thoroughly crushed. If using grinder, grind fruit very fine using small-sectioned cutter. Place combined fruit in jelly bag and let drip for several hours. Or place a dampened square of cheesecloth of four thicknesses over a colander set into a large bowl, pour fruit into cloth, gather ends together and squeeze till all juice is extracted. There should be 3½ cups prepared juice. If a bit short of juice, add a little lemon juice or water to pulp and squeeze again.

Sterilize 8 8-ounce jelly glasses, small-mouth funnel and dipper. Melt 1 bar paraffin.

Measure sugar into a bowl. Measure 3½ cups juice into large cook pot. Mix Sure-Jell with juice in pan. Stir over high heat till mixture boils hard, then stir in sugar at once. Bring to a full rolling boil and *boil hard 1 minute*, stirring constantly. Remove from heat and skim off foam. Remove glasses and invert to drain. Fill hot glasses. Cover at once with melted paraffin. Cool, label and store.

STRAWBERRY JELLY

• If you cannot find rhubarb on your hunting trip, you may make plain strawberry jelly instead, using 2½ quarts of strawberries to obtain the 3½ cups juice. Make the trophy in exactly the same way as instructed for Strawberry-Rhubarb Jelly.

If you missed the strawberry season without going on a hunting trip for the fresh fruit, don't resign yourself to a gift closet minus this delectable berry. Bring down the following trophy that calls for FROZEN strawberry halves, plus a tangy orange.

4. STRAWBERRY-ORANGE JAM

1 medium orange	*¼ cup water*
2 (10 oz.) packages thawed	*3½ cups (1½ lbs.) sugar*
frozen strawberry halves	*½ box Sure-Jell fruit pectin**
(*mix contents of box well; then measure 2½ tablespoons)	

Grate rind of orange; peel off white part of rind and discard. Remove seeds and discard. Cut orange pulp into small pieces; mix with strawberries. Measure 2 2/3 cups of mixture into large cook pot. Add water.

Sterilize 6 8-ounce jelly glasses, wide-mouth funnel and dipper. Melt 1 bar paraffin.

Measure sugar; set aside. Mix Sure-Jell into fruit. Bring to a hard boil over high heat, stirring constantly. *At once* stir in sugar. Bring to a full rolling boil and *boil hard 1 minute,* stirring constantly. Remove from heat; skim off foam with metal spoon. Stir and skim 5 minutes to cool slightly and prevent floating fruit. Remove glasses and invert to drain. Fill glasses. Cover with melted paraffin immediately. Cool, label and store.

19

• Spring is the season to start a delectable trophy known as the Brandied Fruit Melange, once famous in the old South and worthy of renewed fame on your Christmas gift list.

It is really the lazy hunter's dream catch because the labor involved is practically nil, a half-hour to begin it and a few minutes each month to add to its contents until the end of autumn when it can be left alone to "ripen." The melange is begun with the first fruits of the season, usually strawberries, plus brandy, sugar and spices placed in a stone crock which has been scalded with boiling water. At various times other fruits and sugar are added according to the instructions in Trophy #5. Then at some opportune moment before Christmas this remarkable mixture can be sealed in sterilized jars for gift-giving.

A two or four-gallon crock is an ideal container for the melange but any other large wide-mouthed vessel of glass or pottery may be used. *Do not use a metal one.* You may locate a stone crock by calling hardware stores, antique shops, junkyards and similar places.

Brandied Fruit Melange makes an ideal topping for ice cream, puddings, pound cake, crepes, or a garnish for meats.

5. BRANDIED FRUIT MELANGE

*1 quart or 1 pound each of
    fruits in season*
*1 quart good brandy
    (more if needed later)*
1 teaspoon whole cloves

1 2-inch stick cinnamon
*Grated rind of 1 orange
    and 1 lemon*
½ teaspoon ground nutmeg
Granulated sugar
Brown sugar

Scald crock with boiling water. Pour in the brandy; add spices and grated orange and lemon rinds. Add one quart washed and capped strawberries plus 1 cup granulated sugar and 1 cup light brown sugar. Stir carefully. Fit a wad of crumpled aluminum foil inside crock on top of berries. Place a small plate or a saucer on the foil and add a weight such as a clean stone or glass paperweight on the saucer to hold it down. *Do not use a metal weight of any kind.* Weighting the berries down keeps them from floating on top and allows them to become saturated with the melange syrup. Keep the crock in a dark place. If you have to keep the crock in a closet or cellar where dust is a problem, cover the top of the crock with aluminum foil or plastic wrap or a large tight-fitting plate.

When raspberries are in season, add a quart of them plus 1 cup granulated sugar, stir and re-cover. Successively, as they come in season, add cherries, blackberries, diced fresh pineapple, pitted and quartered apricots and plums, peeled, diced peaches and pears, seedless grapes, and other regional fruits that may be available. With each addition, add also 1 cup granulated sugar for each quart or pound of prepared fruit.

If necessary, add more brandy to keep all the fruit covered with melange syrup. If you like a heavier spice flavor, add a bit more spice.

When you have added your last variety of fruit, cover the crock tightly and store for at least two months undisturbed.

At some opportune time before Christmas, estimate the amount of melange you have garnered and the number of jars you will need for individual gifts. Wash and sterilize the proper number of jars of the size you want to use for gifts, and place the same number of lids in one inch of boiling water in a shallow pan for a few minutes. Drain the hot jars on a tray covered with clean paper towels. Let the jars stand inverted until somewhat cooled, then fill them with the melange to within $\frac{1}{2}$ inch of their tops. Seal with the hot lids and screw bands on tightly. Label and store. Any remaining melange will keep in the crock very well, if covered tightly, for months.

Clove   Nutmeg   Cinnamon

• Many hunters stalking through the spring jungle in search of game overlook the succulent rhubarb. True, it is well-known for its use in making delicious pies for it is also called the pieplant.

However, in addition to teaming it up with strawberries in Trophy #3, rhubarb is the main ingredient in the following tasty conserve. Be an adventurous hunter and bring home the ingredients called for in Rhubarb-Raisin Conserve and add this rich bronze trophy to the colors in your gift line-up.

If you are smart enough to save a jar or two for your own use, try making small hot canapes for your Christmas party. Simply place a scant teaspoonful of the conserve on each of as many two-inch rounds of piecrust as you need, dampen edges of each round, and fold over in half-moon shape pressing edges tightly together. Bake in a hot (425 degree) oven until lightly browned. Dust with powdered sugar and serve hot with rolled thin slices of rosy ham and white breast of turkey.

The conserve is equally tasty as a spread for toast, hot biscuits and rolls.

6. RHUBARB-RAISIN CONSERVE

5 lbs. rhubarb
8 cups sugar
2 cups cider vinegar
2 cups seedless raisins
2 oranges (rind and juice)

$\frac{1}{2}$ teaspoon ground cloves
1 teaspoon ground cinnamon
2 cups chopped walnut meats
1 cup liquid from drained
   rhubarb

Wash rhubarb, trim off leaves and root ends, cut stalks in 1-inch pieces and cover with boiling water. Allow to stand 3 minutes; then drain, reserving 1 cup liquid. To the rhubarb, add sugar, vinegar, grated rind and juice of oranges, spices, raisins and the liquid reserved from drained rhubarb. Cook slowly until thickened, stirring often to prevent sticking. To judge when conserve is thick enough, drop a small amount on a cold saucer. If syrup runs freely from the solids, cook longer. Cooking time varies slightly on batches of this recipe, probably due to variation of juice content in rhubarb stalks and/or in the oranges.

While conserve is cooking, sterilize 10 8-ounce jars, wide-mouth funnel and dipper. Sterilize lids.

When conserve is thickened, add nut meats for a last 1 minute of cooking. Using tongs, remove jars and invert to drain. Fill hot jars to within ½ inch of top. Put hot lids on jars; screw bands on tightly. Cool, label and store.

• About this time, red cherries are being brought down by the thousands. Join the game hunters who capture these for a trophy that sparkles on your shelf like scarlet tinsel. Be sure to catch the sour red cherry; do not use the large dark Bing variety.

7. SPARKLING RED CHERRY JELLY

3 lbs. sour red ripe cherries
3 lbs. sugar (7 cups)
½ cup water

6 crushed cherry pits (meats)
1 bottle Certo fruit pectin

Remove stems from cherries, wash and drain. Pit only six of them. Tie the 6 pits in a small square of cheesecloth and crush with hammer. Remove meats, discarding shells. Place cherries in large cook pot. Crush with potato masher or bottom of heavy cup. (Or place in heavy plastic bag that contains no air holes, close top with rubber band, and crush.) Add the 6 pit meats and ½ cup water to crushed cherries in pot, bring to boil and simmer for ten minutes, covered.

Place a square of cheesecloth of four thicknesses over a colander set in a large bowl and ladle cherries into center of cheesecloth. Cool to handling temperature, gather ends of cloth together, and squeeze and twist to extract juice. If you are *very* particular and have the time, you may use a jelly bag and let fruit drip for several hours or overnight; however, in this case you must use an extra 1½ lbs. of cherries to obtain the required amount of juice.

You should have at least 3½ cups juice, but if you are a bit short of this total you may add a small amount of boiling water to fruit pulp and squeeze again.

Sterilize 8 8-ounce jelly glasses or baby-food jars, small-mouth funnel and dipper. Melt 1 bar paraffin.

Mix sugar and juice in large cook pot and heat to boiling while stirring with long-handled spoon. As soon as mixture boils, stir in the Certo fruit pectin.

While the mixture reheats to a full rolling boil, quickly remove jelly glasses from hot water and invert to drain.

When jelly comes to a full rolling boil, *boil hard for 1 minute,* stirring constantly. Remove from heat, skim off foam with metal spoon, and fill hot glasses. Cover jelly immediately with melted paraffin. Cool, label and store.

24

• Add a touch of sunshine to your gift shelf by capturing the following trophy that calls for little golden apricots. Blend the apricots with canned crushed pineapple for a delicious marmalade that glows on hot breads or toast, and try it also as a filling between thin slices of pound cake, a topping for cottage cheese, or a touch of sparkle in peanut butter sandwiches.

8. APRICOT-PINEAPPLE MARMALADE

1 lemon, medium size	2 lbs. ripe apricots
1 orange, medium size	1 lb. 4 oz. can crushed
¾ cup water	pineapple
Dash (¹⁄₁₆ teaspoon)	5 cups sugar
baking soda	1 box Sure-Jell fruit pectin

Remove rinds from lemon and orange, discarding half the white part of rinds. Chop or grind remaining rinds finely. Add water and baking soda to rinds in 1½-quart pot, bring to a boil, and simmer, *covered,* 10 minutes, stirring often. Chop peeled fruit of orange and lemon, discarding seeds; add to rinds and simmer 20 minutes longer. Pit (do not peel) the apricots, cut or chop into small pieces, and combine with rinds. Add pineapple. Measure 4½ cups fruit into large cook pot.

Sterilize 9 8-ounce jelly glasses, wide-mouth funnel and dipper. Melt 1 bar of paraffin.

Measure sugar into bowl and set aside. Mix Sure-Jell pectin into fruit. Bring to a hard boil over high heat, stirring constantly; then *cook gently 1 minute. At once* stir in sugar.

While the mixture reheats to a full rolling boil, quickly remove jelly glasses from hot water and invert to drain.

When marmalade comes to a full rolling boil, *boil hard 1 minute,* stirring constantly. Remove from heat; skim off foam with metal spoon. Then stir and skim 5 minutes to cool slightly and prevent floating fruit. Fill jelly glasses. Cover marmalade immediately with melted paraffin. Cool, label and store.

• Feel in the mood for hunting a most unusual trophy? Does your local hunting ground occasionally offer a "special" on ripe bananas? Meaning the lightly-speckled but still firm stage of the fruit when it is packed with rich, sugary flavor that must be caught before another day over-ripens it. Take advantage of this goodness at a price bargain.

9. BANANA BUTTER

About 10 bananas
(3 cups fruit)
Juice of 1 lemon
(2 tablespoons)

$\frac{1}{3}$ cup finely chopped
    maraschino cherries
$6\frac{1}{2}$ cups sugar
1 bottle Certo fruit pectin

Mash bananas thoroughly. Measure 3 cups into large cook pot and add lemon juice and cherries. Add sugar and mix well.

Sterilize 9 8-ounce jelly glasses or baby-food jars, wide-mouth funnel and dipper. Melt 1 bar of paraffin.

Bring fruit mixture to boil over high heat, stirring constantly. When it comes to a full rolling boil, *boil hard 1 minute,* then remove from heat and *at once* stir in Certo fruit pectin.

Remove glasses from hot water, inverting to drain. Fill immediately with banana butter. Cover at once with melted paraffin. Cool, label and store.

• Now, fellow-hunters, you may pause in your labors, and take a little time to gloat over that Spring shelf. But for goodness' sake don't brag about your prowess to your friends. They'll try to take home some of your hard-earned booty. Anyway, isn't a Christmas gift supposed to be a surprise?

This is a good time to check your supplies of ammunition, such as jars, paraffin, sugar, fruit pectin and labels. Jot down any items which need replenishing so you won't have to trust your memory on your next trip to the Supermart Woods. Don't wait till summer arrives. Someone may suddenly gift you with the overabundance of their peach tree or cucumber patch and catch you with your gun unloaded.

26

Chapter **III**

Summer is Coming

On to Peaches

Sitting on your patio, fanning and complaining of the heat? Hard to get rolling? Sing "Deck the Halls, etc." and think of Christmas while downing a tot of frosty mint tea.

Of course, if you are fortunate in having air conditioning you may not need the tea. If you own a record-player AND good old Bing's platter of "White Christmas," you are doubly fortunate; you can dispense with your own singing and save your energy for a hunting expedition to the wilds of your favorite Supermart Woods.

The flavor of the following luscious concoction is beyond description. Try it with hot scones, as a topping for a heavenly sundae, or as a filling for tiny little tarts.

27

10. PEACH-MARASCHINO CONSERVE

3½ lbs. ripe peaches
  ½ cup maraschino cherries,
    chopped
  5 cups sugar

⅛ teaspoon salt
Juice of 1 medium lemon
Juice of 1 medium orange
1 cup chopped nutmeats

Drop washed peaches into boiling water for 1 minute, remove with tongs and drop into cold water. Skins should slip off readily. Remove pits and chop fruit finely. Should measure about 5 cups fruit. Drain juice from chopped cherries, and put peaches and cherry juice into a large cook pot. Add sugar, salt, juice of lemon and orange, and stir over low heat until sugar dissolves. Turn up heat and boil, stirring often, until syrup thickens (when a few thick drops run together when dropped from tip of spoon.) This should take about 35 minutes.

Stir in the finely chopped cherries and chopped nuts, then bring back to a boil. Turn off heat and let stand for several hours or overnight. Stir occasionally for the first hour.

In the morning, or at least five hours later, reheat the conserve to a boil, stirring often. While conserve is reheating, sterilize 6 8-ounce jars, lids, wide-mouth funnel and dipper.

When conserve boils, remove jars from hot water with tongs and invert to drain. Fill jars. Place lids on jars. Screw bands on tightly. Cool, label and store.

• A variation of Trophy #10 calls for the addition of nuts and pineapple and a different hunting method with the help of Certo fruit pectin. This trophy may be captured in either 8-ounce canning jars or jelly glasses.

11. CALICO PEACH-PINEAPPLE CONSERVE

2¼ cups prepared ripe peaches
⅓ cup chopped maraschino
    cherries
1 small can (8½ oz.) crushed
    pineapple

¼ cup lemon juice (2 lemons)
1½ cups chopped nuts
7½ cups sugar
1 bottle Certo fruit pectin

Drop fully ripe peaches into boiling water for 1 minute, then into cold water. Skins will peel off easily. Remove pits and chop or grind fruit. Measure 2¼ cups into large cook pot. Add chopped cherries, pineapple, lemon juice and nuts. Add sugar to fruit and mix well.

Sterilize 10 8-ounce canning jars or jelly glasses, wide-mouth funnel, dipper and lids. If using jelly glasses, melt 2 bars of paraffin.

Place conserve mixture over high heat; bring to full rolling boil and *boil hard for 1 minute,* stirring constantly. Remove from heat and *at once* stir in Certo fruit pectin. Skim off foam. Then stir and skim for 5 minutes to cool slightly and prevent floating fruit.

While cooling the conserve slightly, remove hot jars or glasses from boiling water and invert to drain. Fill jars or glasses. Place lids on jars; screw bands on tightly. Or, if using jelly glasses, cover with melted paraffin. Cool, label and store.

• The season for red raspberries is short; moreover, many sections of the country seldom see more than a few boxes of these little critters in their local Supermart Woods. The smart hunter will not give up the joy of capturing their unique flavor in a trophy, but will use frozen red raspberries to add a lovely rosy glow to the following peach jam.

29

12. PEACH-RASPBERRY JAM

1 10-oz. package frozen red
  raspberries, thawed
  (1¼ cups)
2¾ cups prepared ripe peaches

¼ cup lemon juice (2 lemons)
6 cups sugar
½ bottle Certo fruit pectin

Drop fully ripe peaches into boiling water for 1 minute, then into cold water. Skins will peel off easily. Remove and discard pits and crush fruit finely.

Measure thawed raspberries; add crushed peaches to make 4 cups. Combine fruit and lemon juice in very large cook pot. Stir sugar into fruit.

Sterilize 9 8-ounce canning jars or jelly glasses, wide-mouth funnel and dipper. Sterilize lids or, if using jelly glasses, melt 1 bar of paraffin.

Place jam mixture over high heat, bring to a full rolling boil and *boil hard for 1 minute,* stirring constantly. Remove from heat; *at once* stir in Certo fruit pectin. Skim off foam with metal spoon. Then stir and skim 5 minutes to cool slightly and prevent floating fruit.

While cooling jam, remove hot jars or glasses and invert to drain.

Fill jars or glasses. Place lids on jars; screw bands on tightly. Or, if using jelly glasses, cover with melted paraffin. Cool, label and store.

PEAR-RASPBERRY JAM

When pears become plentiful in the fall, they may be used instead of peaches in the foregoing recipe, in the same amount. About 2 pounds of peeled and cored pears will measure 2¾ cups prepared fruit. Pear-Raspberry Jam's delightful flavor is enhanced by the addition of 1 to 2 tablespoons grated orange rind to the lemon juice in the trophy.

• One lovely color demands its complement, so when you've recovered from your recent hunting labors you can repeat your sharpshooting artistry with this one. Delicious teamed with roast beef, ham or turkey.

13. PEACH CHUTNEY (1)

7 cups firm ripe peaches
    (about 5 lbs.)
2½ cups sugar
  1 cup chopped Bermuda
      onion
  1 large clove garlic, minced
      (or ½ teaspoon garlic
      powder)
¼ cup Worcestershire sauce
1½ cups cider vinegar

1 cup dried currants
    (rinsed and drained)
1 small pod chili pepper
    (or ½ teaspoon
    Tabasco)
1 teaspoon ground ginger
1 stick cinnamon and
1 teaspoon whole allspice
    (tied in cheesecloth bag)

Peel peaches, pit and slice into ¼ inch thick pieces lengthwise. Measure 7 cups peaches into a large bowl, cover with 1 quart ice water and 2 tablespoons salt. Cover and let stand overnight.

In the morning, mix all ingredients *except the peaches* in a large cook pot and boil for ten minutes. Then add peaches and boil gently, stirring often, until fruit is clear and syrup thickened.

While cooking the chutney, sterilize 7 8-ounce jars, lids, wide-mouth funnel and dipper.

When chutney has reached the proper consistency (fruit clear, syrup fairly thick) remove spice bag. Remove jars from hot water, and invert to drain. Fill jars to within ¼ inch of top. Remove lids from hot water and place on jars. Screw bands on tight. Cool, label and store.

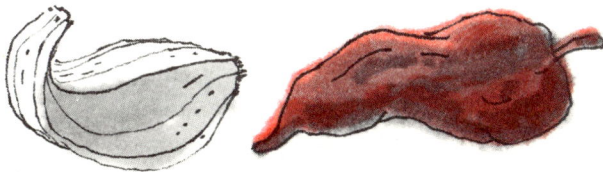

• An American version of Peach Chutney, Trophy #14, is a bit sweeter, and calls for the use of Sure-Jell fruit pectin, raisins in place of currants, and other minor variations.

It can be captured in less time than the first since the peaches need not be "hardened" overnight in brine and are therefore softer than those in the Indian type chutney, and the boiling time is cut to 5 minutes.

NECTARINE CHUTNEY

Firm ripe nectarines may be substituted for firm ripe peaches in either version. Do not use fully ripe soft fruit for this becomes too mushy in the cooking.

14. PEACH CHUTNEY (2)

4 cups firm ripe peaches (about 3 lbs.)	1 tablespoon salt
	1 teaspoon ground allspice
½ cup vinegar	½ teaspoon each ground
¼ cup lemon juice (2 lemons)	cinnamon, cloves, and ginger
1 cup seedless raisins	¾ cup firmly packed
¼ cup slivered preserved ginger	brown sugar
	4½ cups granulated sugar
⅓ cup chopped onion	1 box Sure-Jell fruit pectin

Peel and pit firm ripe peaches, cut in small squares, and measure 4 cups into a large cook pot. Add drained slivered ginger and all the other ingredients *except the sugars*. Mix thoroughly. Measure sugars; set aside. Add Sure-Jell fruit pectin to fruit; mix well.

Sterilize 10 8-ounce jars and lids, or 10 8-ounce jelly glasses, wide-mouth funnel and dipper. If using glasses, melt 2 bars of paraffin.

Place fruit over high heat; stir until mixture comes to a hard boil. *At once* stir in sugars. Bring to a full rolling boil and *boil hard for 5 minutes,* stirring constantly. Remove from heat; skim off foam with metal spoon. Stir and skim for 10 minutes to cool slightly and prevent floating fruit.

While cooling chutney slightly, remove hot jars or glasses from boiling water and invert on a tray. Fill jars or glasses. Place lids on jars; screw bands on tightly. Or, if using jelly glasses, cover with melted paraffin. Cool, label and store.

• The versatile peach combines with many flavors for a variety of uses. For an excellent dessert topping, especially on ice cream, or a sprightly spread for hot breads, this is a taste sensation.

15. PEACH·RUM JAM

4 cups fully ripe peaches   ¼ cup dark Jamaica rum
    (about 3 lbs.)   1 box Sure·Jell fruit pectin
5 cups sugar

Drop peaches into boiling water, then into cold water. Peel, pit, and chop or grind very fine. Measure 4 cups into a large cook pot. Measure sugar and set aside. Add rum and Sure·Jell fruit pectin to fruit and mix well.

Sterilize 9 8·ounce jelly glasses, wide·mouth funnel and dipper. Melt 1 bar of paraffin.

Place fruit over high heat and stir until mixture comes to a hard boil. *At once* stir in sugar. Bring to a full rolling boil and *boil hard 1 minute,* stirring constantly. Remove from heat and skim off foam with metal spoon. Then stir and skim for 5 minutes to cool slightly and prevent floating fruit.

While skimming, remove hot glasses from boiling water and invert to drain. Fill glasses and wipe any spills from rims with paper towel dipped in boiling water. Cover at once with hot paraffin. Cool, label and store.

• By now, summer is well along. Cantaloupe should be plentiful, so why not add the golden glow of this delectable conserve to your summer shelf? Don't let the requirement of blanched almonds or filberts for this recipe stop you. If you can't locate nuts in their shells in the summertime at the Supermart Woods, you can always use the canned or packaged nuts, already blanched and sliced for you.

But if you have nuts in the shell on hand and want to prepare them yourself, simply shell the required amount, boil in a little water for about five minutes, drain, cover with cold water and then slip the skins right off. Sliver or chop into pieces.

This easy-to-make trophy is extremely popular among my "giftees" and I've had requests for extra jars for special occasions all during the year. Be hard-hearted if this happens to you. Saving this conserve for a Christmas special will up your status as a star gift-giver!

16. PEACH-CANTALOUPE CONSERVE

4 cups prepared cantaloupe
   (2 medium)
4 cups prepared ripe peaches
   (about 3 lbs.)
6 cups sugar
1/4 cup fresh lemon juice
   (2 lemons)

1/2 teaspoon nutmeg
1 teaspoon grated lemon rind
3/4 cup slivered blanched
   almonds or chopped
   filberts

Drop peaches into boiling water for 1 minute, then into cold water. Peel off skins and pit fruit. Pare cantaloupe. Grate rind of 1 lemon and squeeze juice of 2 lemons. Chop peaches and cantaloupe coarsely and measure 8 cups combined fruit into a large cook pot. Add lemon juice.

Bring to boil, stirring occasionally. Add sugar, stirring until it dissolves and mixture boils again. Then boil for twenty minutes, or until fruit becomes transparent, stirring occasionally.

While conserve is cooking, sterilize 8 8-ounce jars and lids,

34

wide-mouth funnel and dipper.

When fruit has become transparent, add the nutmeg, grated lemon rind and blanched slivered almonds or chopped filberts. Boil 3 minutes longer, stirring as needed.

While boiling the mixture, remove jars from boiling water and invert to drain.

When conserve is ready, fill the hot jars to within $1/4$ inch of rims. Place lids on jars. Screw bands on tightly. Cool, label and store.

• Enthusiastic hunters who brought down more peaches and cantaloupes than were needed in the preparation of Trophy #16 will be happy to use their excess fruit to acquire the following marvelous marmalade.

It differs from the conserve in the addition of crushed pineapple, the omission of nuts and nutmeg, and in chopping the fruit in small pieces instead of coarse ones.

Snow-white layers of cake put together with a filling of this rich marmalade makes a dessert that even a mother-in-law can't find wrong. Ice cream topped with its golden shimmer makes a dish fit for visiting royalty.

17. PEACH-PI-CANTALOUPE MARMALADE

1 14-oz. can (1¾ cups) crushed pineapple
2 cups prepared peaches (about 1½ lbs.)
3 cups prepared cantaloupe
6 cups granulated sugar
3 tablespoons lemon juice

Drop peaches into boiling water for 1 minute, then into cold water. Peel off skins and pit fruit. Pare cantaloupe. Squeeze lemon juice. Chop peaches and cantaloupe finely. Measure 2 cups peaches and 3 cups cantaloupe into large cook pot, add pineapple (drained) and bring to a boil. Stir frequently. Boil gently until juice begins to thicken and fruit becomes transparent, about 10-15 minutes.

While marmalade mixture is cooking sterilize 7 8-ounce jars

and lids, wide-mouth funnel and dipper.

When fruit is transparent, slowly add the sugar, a cup at a time, boiling the mixture gently and stirring till sugar is dissolved. Boil 5 minutes longer, then add lemon juice. Continue boiling and stirring frequently until juice begins to jell. When two drops run together at the tip of a spoon in a kind of "sheet" the marmalade is ready. Should take about 30 minutes. Remove from heat.

Remove hot jars from boiling water, invert to drain, then fill with marmalade to within 1/4 inch of top. Place lids on jars. Screw bands on tightly. Cool, label and store.

• Have you ever eyed the scads of cool green cucumbers just waiting to be picked off their perches by any Nimrod with ammunition? Eyed them wistfully, that is, because you believe that all recipes for turning them into delectable concoctions are too complicated for you to tackle?

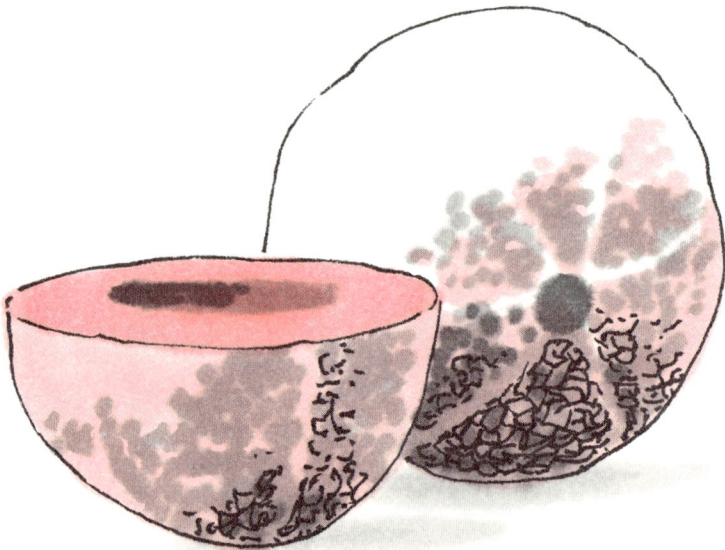

Eye no more, but take aim and bag a few baskets because you are hereby being presented with three trophies that are paragons of good taste, simple, easy and foolproof.

There's no better way to highlight the long hot season of hunt-ing than by adding these marvelous gold-green triumphs to your shelf of summer beauties.

18. EASY CUCUMBER CRISPS

9 medium cucumbers	2 cups sugar
2 tablespoons salt	1 teaspoon dry mustard
Crushed ice or ice cubes	$\frac{1}{2}$ teaspoon turmeric
6 medium onions	$2\frac{1}{2}$ teaspoons mustard seed
1 quart cider vinegar	$2\frac{1}{2}$ teaspoons celery seed

Wash cucumbers thoroughly. Trim ends. Pare a narrow strip down each side lengthwise, and slice thinly (not quite paper-thin). Slices should measure from $2\frac{1}{2}$ to 3 quarts. Cover with salt and crushed ice or ice cubes and let soak for 3 or 4 hours. Then drain well.

While draining cucumbers in colander or large strainer, sterilize 12 8-ounce jars and lids, wide-mouth funnel and dipper.

Remove brown skins from onions while holding them under running cold water. Thinly slice onions. A burnt kitchen match held in mouth, burnt end out, will absorb some of the onion fumes. Mix together all the spices and seeds in a cup.

Put the drained cucumber slices and onion slices in a large cook pot, add vinegar, sugar, spices and seeds, mix well and bring to a boil.

While waiting for the crisps to boil, remove jars from boiling water and invert to drain.

When crisps come to a boil, stir and boil for *only fifteen seconds, no longer!* Remove from heat and fill hot jars to within $\frac{1}{4}$ inch of tops. Place lids on jars. Screw bands on tightly. Cool, label and store.

37

19. CUCUMBER MARMALADE

2 cups (about 1½ lbs.)
   prepared cucumbers
4 cups sugar
⅓ cup lemon juice
   (about 3 lemons)

2 tablespoons grated lemon
   rind
Few drops green food
   coloring (optional)
½ bottle Certo fruit pectin

Wash and peel cucumbers; chop very fine. Measure 2 cups in a large cook pot. Add sugar, lemon juice and grated rind; mix well.

Sterilize 5 8-ounce jars and lids, or 5 8-ounce jelly glasses, wide-mouth funnel and dipper. If using glasses, melt 1 bar paraffin.

Place cucumber mixture over high heat, add food coloring, bring to a full rolling boil and *boil hard 1 minute*, stirring constantly. Remove from heat; *at once*, stir in Certo fruit pectin. Skim off foam with metal spoon. Then stir and skim 5 minutes to prevent floating particles.

While skimming, remove hot jars or glasses from boiling water and invert to drain. Fill jars or glasses. Remove jar lids from hot water and place on jars; screw bands on tightly. Or, if using jelly glasses, cover with melted paraffin. Cool, label and store.

20. CUCUMBER RELISH

8 cups chopped cucumbers
   (about 6 lbs.)
1 cup chopped onion
   (4 medium)
2 cups chopped red sweet
   peppers (6 medium)
2 cups chopped green sweet
   peppers (6 medium)

1 tablespoon turmeric
½ cup salt
1 tablespoon mustard seed
2 sticks cinnamon
1 teaspoon cloves
2 teaspoons allspice
1 to 2 cups brown sugar
4 cups vinegar

Wash and drain vegetable. Peel onions; remove seeds from peppers. Chop and measure all vegetables, place in large cook pot. Sprinkle turmeric over vegetables. Dissolve salt in 8 cups cool water; pour over vegetables, and let stand 3 to 4 hours. Drain.

Cover vegetables with cool water. Let stand 1 hour. Drain. Measure vinegar into large cook pot, add spices (tied in cheese-cloth or muslin bag) and sugar to vinegar. Heat to boiling. Pour over vegetables, cover and let stand *12 to 18 hours* at room tem-perature. Next day, simmer relish mixture until hot through. If it seems dry, add a little more vinegar. Bring to boiling.

While mixture is heating slowly, sterilize 12 8-ounce jars and lids, wide-mouth funnel and dipper. Remove jars from boiling water (when relish is ready) and invert to drain.

When relish boils, stir and boil for *fifteen seconds, no longer*. Remove from heat. Fill hot jars to within $1/4$ inch of tops. Remove lids from hot water and place on jars. Screw bands on tightly. Cool, label and store.

NOTE: This recipe may be cut in half; however, the times for soaking and standing remain the same. If you prefer a sweeter relish, use the two cups brown sugar; if you prefer a relish on the sour side, use only one cup.

• The image of bountiful summer on your gift shelf is not com-plete without the capture of either blackberry or blueberry beauty; either will add a rich blue-purple color to your rainbow of goodies.

21. OLD-TIME BLACKBERRY JAM

3 quarts blackberries   *3 cups sugar*

Wash firm ripe blackberries, drain thoroughly, place in a large cook pot and mash. Place pot over a low flame and heat thor-oughly. Press hot fruit through a sieve to remove seeds.

Measure pulp and liquid. There should be about 3 pints. Add one cup sugar for every pint of pulp. Return to heat and cook rapidly until thick, stirring to prevent burning.

Sterilize 7 8-ounce jars and lids, wide-mouth funnel and dipper.

When jam has thickened, remove from heat. Drain the hot jars and fill to within $1/4$ inch of tops. Remove lids from hot water and place on jars. Screw on bands tightly. Cool, label and store.

22. BLUEBERRY MARMALADE

3 cups prepared fruit (1 orange, 1 lemon, 1 full pint cultivated
blueberries)

5 cups granulated sugar   *¾ cup water*
½ bottle Certo fruit pectin   *⅛ teaspoon soda*

Remove skins in quarters from 1 medium orange and 1 medium lemon. Lay quarters flat; shave off and discard about half of white part. With sharp knife or scissors, slice remaining rind very fine, or chop or grind. Add ¾ cup water and ⅛ teaspoon soda; bring to boil and simmer, *covered,* 10 minutes, stirring occasionally.

Chop the peeled fruit, discarding seeds. Add pulp and juice to undrained cooked rind, and simmer, *covered,* 15 minutes longer. Crush thoroughly 1 pint fully ripe cultivated blueberries. Combine fruits and measure 3 cups into a very large cook pot.

Sterilize 6 8-ounce jelly glasses, wide-mouth funnel and dipper. Melt 1 bar of paraffin.

Add sugar to fruit in cook pot, mix well, and bring to a full rolling boil. *Boil hard 1 minute,* stirring constantly. Remove from heat and *at once* stir in Certo fruit pectin. Skim off foam with metal spoon. Then stir and skim by turns for 5 minutes to cool slightly, to prevent floating fruit. Remove glasses from hot water and invert to drain. Fill with marmalade to within ¼ inch of tops. Cover with paraffin. Cool, label and store.

• Few modern hunters want to bother with the complicated pro-cedure our grandmothers used to capture the goodness of pre-

served watermelon rind. Nowadays, the good white part of the melon disappears in the garbage pail or disposal without a house-wifely qualm.

However, now that I show you how to bring down *easily* a most delicious trophy, one that will spread your breakfast toast or hot muffins with a golden summer fragrance even in the wintertime, there is no longer any excuse for such waste.

If your family is small and eats only a few slices of watermelon at a meal, or if you buy the "apartment-size" small watermelons, you may keep the peeled and trimmed portions of the rind in a plastic bag in your refrigerator for a few days, adding more rind as the melon or small melons are eaten each day, until you have the required amount for the trophy.

23. WATERMELON RIND HONEY

6 cups peeled, trimmed watermelon rind	1/2 teaspoon ginger
	1/2 teaspoon whole cloves
1 cup water	2 two-inch sticks cinnamon
6 cups sugar	1/4 teaspoon salt
6 slices lemon	

Wash and pare green outer rind and red meat from rind and discard. Put white rind through food chopper, using coarse blade. Measure 6 cups. Place in a cook pot with 1 cup water. Cook slowly, uncovered, until melon is clear, stirring occasionally, about 25 minutes.

Thinly slice lemon. Tie spices in cheesecloth bag. Add sugar, lemon, spices and salt to the melon. Stir and cook slowly until thickened, 1 hour and 15 minutes. Remove spice bag.

About 20 minutes before the honey is ready, sterilize 5 8-ounce jars and lids, wide-mouth funnel and dipper.

When honey has finished cooking, fill the drained hot jars to within 1/4 inch of tops. Remove jar lids from hot water, place on jars, screw bands on tightly. Cool, label and store.

41

Chapter IV

Autumn Daze

And Apples

Ah, October's bright blue weather, and that wine of which the poets sing is in the air! Now that your summer booty has been stashed away, enjoy the wine but keep track of the days left for hunting. Don't wait till winter to stock up on canning jars, lids, paraffin, sugar and such. Except for the sugar, merchants seldom restock their shelves with canning equipment once the hunting seasons have passed. And there is nothing more frustrating than to latch on to some priceless trophy-guidance (such as you will find in the following pages) only to discover that you cannot buy the ammunition needed to capture a last-minute addition to your gift closet. Check your hunting supplies *now!*

Sometime during the fall, acquire a 3 to 4 pound pumpkin. It will be a festive color accent on your fall dining table or in your kitchen for a few weeks, and eventually you will have it available for use in a wonderful conserve, to be captured after you have taken advantage of the earlier fruits of this season.

42

Another reminder. Have you been keeping that list of acquired trophies up to date? Don't forget to add the latest acquisitions and to deduct any that you haven't been able to resist using. Even one missing goodie may cause a gap in your Christmas apportioning, and you'll lament over the one that isn't there more than over the one that got away.

Now forget the wine in the air, and open the season's first keg of cider and a bottle of brandy — not for sampling, sorry, but to help capture this always-welcome critter, the full mincemeat crock.

This trophy is pretty old. I conned the directions for capturing it from a fellow-marksman while we were on jury duty years ago, and she claimed her family inherited these directions from a Colonial Dame who hunted with Daniel Boone's grandmother. No matter, I guarantee that whoever tastes this magnificent mixture will be forever young and starry-eyed throughout the holidays. A jar of it makes a truly patrician gift. Compared to this mincemeat, the pallid concoctions available to less fortunate gourmets are peasant ersatz.

The first step is to lay in your ammunition, not the least of which is a container large enough to hold all the ingredients with room left over to stir them up occasionally. The ideal container is a 4-gallon stone crock, an item seldom found in the average household these days. However, you can probably locate a few at places like junkyards, hardware stores, or antique shops. All the other ingredients can be obtained at liquor stores, supermarts or grocery stores.

I hope you remembered to save several instant-coffee jars as I advised in an earlier chapter. Each jar holds almost a quart of mincemeat, just the right amount for a large pie. If you must make your supply of mincemeat stretch over a larger list of giftees, you can use pint-sized jars which hold enough for small pies.

One last tip before beginning your hunt. You may want to take advantage of a bonus connected with the apples needed for this trophy. Turn to page 45 to learn about this economy.

24. BELLE FLOWER'S MINCEMEAT

2 lbs. lean beef
2 lbs. seedless raisins
2 lbs. Sultana (white) raisins
2 lbs. currants
½ lb. citron
2 teaspoons ground nutmeg
2 teaspoons ground cloves
2 teaspoons mace
4 teaspoons ground cinnamon
2 lbs. beef suet

½ lb. candied lemon peel
4 lbs. apples
2 lbs. sugar
1 teaspoon salt
2 oranges
2 lemons
1 cup white rum
1 quart sherry or currant
    wine
1 quart good brandy

plus additional half-pint each of sherry and cider, to be added
two or three weeks later after first brandy is absorbed.

Cover the meat with boiling water and simmer gently until tender. Cool. Shred the suet or chop into small squares. Pare, core and chop apples. Shred citron. Grate rinds of oranges and lemons, and squeeze juice.

When the meat is cold, pour off liquid (use liquid for soup or stew; it can be frozen for use later). Grind the meat, mix with chopped suet, citron, apples, raisins and lemon peel. Mix sugar with salt and ground spices, stir through meat and fruit, and add juice and rind of oranges and lemons. Mix well, and add rum, brandy and the quart of sherry. Store crock away in a cool place, covered with lid (if your crock has one) or with aluminum foil or Saran wrap. After two or three weeks, add a half-pint each of cider and sherry and mix well again. If mixture seems too thick after a month, add a bit more cider. Mincemeat made by this recipe will keep in the crock all winter.

After the mincemeat has ripened for a month in the crock, it may be divided up into jars for gift-giving. If you know that your recipient will use the mincemeat within a few months, you will not have to sterilize or seal the jars. You may use clean instant-coffee jars, mayonnaise or pickle jars. Simply fill the clean jars, add a tablespoon of brandy or sherry on top, and screw on the regular coffee jar or other lids.

However, if the mincemeat is to be held longer than six months before using, it will keep best if the containers are sterilized and sealed. Large instant coffee jars have the same size rims as canning jars, so you may use the canning lids and bands. The large coffee jar, originally containing six dry ounces of instant coffee, will hold twenty-four liquid ounces of mincemeat, which is just enough to fill a 9-inch piecrust. Pint-sized jars, such as mayonnaise or pickle jars, hold enough mincemeat to fill a 7-inch piecrust. One admonition: if you intend to sterilize and seal pint-sized containers, use regular pint canning jars; some mayonnaise and pickle jar rims are smaller than canning lids, and will not seal tightly.

To prepare sealed jars, first scald the jars in boiling water for five minutes. Heat as much mincemeat as you wish to put into jars until it comes to the boiling point. Keep the flame low and stir mixture often so it will not scorch. When it comes to a boil, ladle into the hot jars. Heat the canning lids in one inch of boiling water in a shallow pan for a few minutes, remove with tongs, and place on the jars. Holding hot jars with oven mitt or clean tea towel, screw bands on tightly. Cool, label and store.

• Experienced hunters know that apples have marvelous jelly-making qualities, and trophies containing their juice are among the easiest to acquire. Although plain apple jelly is a good old standby, combinations with other fruit juices give delicious novelty flavors that pep up the gift collection.

Before begining the hunt for these varieties, let your guide pass on to you a bonus saving lurking in the apple trophy field.

When acquiring a trophy that calls for the addition of peeled, cored apples (such as Belle Flower's Mincemeat and Tomato-Apple Chutney) do not discard the cores and skins of these apples. Instead, simmer them with a little water (about two cups of water to four cups of peels and cores) for ten minutes, crush thoroughly, simmer five minutes longer, and press out juice through four thicknesses of dampened cheesecloth spread over a colander set in a large bowl. This apple juice may be reserved in the refrigerator for a day or so until you want to use it in a combination jelly such as Tutti-Frutti, Rose Vanilla or Honey-Fruit.

This no-waste bonus may seem a small economy if one is fortunate in owning a bountiful apple tree, but for those of us who must pay by the pound for apples in the Supermart Woods, the saving can mean acquiring the very best apples instead of those of poor grade or taste. It also means a saving of time because one peels and cores only one batch of apples for two trophies!

NOTE: this juice is recommended for use only in trophies calling for the addition of powdered or liquid fruit pectin.

25. ROSE VANILLA JELLY

5 cups sugar
4 cups apple juice (canned, bottled, or "bonus" apple juice prepared according to direction on preceding page)
Few drops red food coloring for rosy hue
2 teaspoons pure vanilla   1 box Sure-Jell fruit pectin
extract

Sterilize 8 8-ounce jelly glasses, small-mouth funnel and dipper. Melt 1 bar of paraffin.

Now measure sugar and set aside. Measure juice into a large cook pot, add red food coloring and vanilla, and then stir in Sure-Jell powdered fruit pectin, mixing well. Bring to a hard boil over high heat, stirring constantly. *At once* stir in sugar. Stirring constantly, bring to a full rolling boil and *boil hard for 1 minute.* Remove from heat and skim off foam with metal spoon.

Drain hot glasses, then fill with the jelly. Cover jelly with melted paraffin. Cool, label and store.

*   *   *

CIDER JELLY: Prepare as for Rose Vanilla Jelly, decreasing sugar to 4½ cups and using cider instead of apple juice. Omit vanilla; substitute 2 tablespoons red cinnamon candies for color and spicy flavor.

46

• Is there someone on your Christmas gift list who is simply mad about herbs, who discourses on the merits of tarragon versus thyme or marjoram, and who will not consider any dish well prepared without a soupçon of additional herb seasoning?

The following trophy is a natural and is a tasty jelly that anyone else will enjoy, too. Try it on tiny biscuits at Sunday brunch, as a pretty red or green touch with sliced Christmas turkey or ham, and as an extra filler in cream-cheese sandwiches.

The best thing about this trophy is that you may choose any one of a dozen different herbs, according to the preferences of your recipients. One batch will make two kinds of Herb-Apple Jelly; for example, five glasses of green-hued Mint and five more of sparkling red Tarragon.

26. APPLE-HERB JELLY

For one batch: to be divided to make two kinds of herb jelly

4 lbs. tart ripe apples   *6½ cups water*

Wash apples; cut in eighths. Place in large cook pot and add 6½ cups water. Bring to boil; simmer, *covered,* 10 minutes, or until apples are soft. Crush with masher; simmer, *covered,* 5 minutes longer. Strain through four thicknesses of cheesecloth over a colander set in a large bowl, pressing and squeezing till all juice is extracted. There should be about 5 cups. If the amount is slightly short, add a little more hot water to pulp and press out again.

For each 2½ cups apple juice:

¼ cup dried herb (either   *4 cups sugar*
tarragon, thyme,   *Few drops red or green*
marjoram, basil, mint,   *food coloring*
sage or savory)   *½ bottle Certo fruit pectin*
¼ cup vinegar

Measure 2½ cups juice into small cook pot. Bring to a boil and pour over dried herb. Let stand 15 minutes; strain through cheesecloth. Place juice in large cook pot; add $\frac{1}{4}$ cup vinegar and 4 cups sugar; mix well. Place over high heat and bring to a boil.

While mixture is coming to a boil, sterilize 5 8-ounce jelly glasses, small-mouth funnel and dipper. Melt 1 bar of paraffin.

When mixture comes to a boil, add $\frac{1}{2}$ bottle Certo fruit pectin and a few drops of either red or green food coloring. Stirring constantly, bring to a full rolling boil, *boil hard 1 minute*, and remove from heat. Skim off foam with metal spoon.

Remove the hot jelly glasses and invert to drain. Fill with the jelly. Cover jelly with melted paraffin. Cool, label and store.

Now repeat, using the remaining $2\frac{1}{2}$ cups apple juice and a different herb and coloring, to make 5 glasses more.

• This pink-tinted relish makes a trophy as pretty as it is tasty. No peeling of the apples is called for so it is easy and quick to capture. Serve it with meats or as a spread.

27. APPLE RELISH

4 cups prepared apples	*Few drops red food*
(about 3 lbs.)	*coloring (optional)*
7 cups sugar	*$\frac{1}{2}$ cup finely chopped nuts*
$\frac{1}{2}$ cup vinegar	*$\frac{1}{2}$ cup seedless raisins*
	$\frac{1}{2}$ bottle Certo fruit pectin

Core and grind unpeeled ripe apples. Measure 4 cups into a large cook pot. Add sugar, vinegar, nuts, and raisins to fruit. Mix well. Add red food coloring if desired to make a pale pink tint.

Sterilize 10 8-ounce jelly glasses, wide-mouth funnel and dipper. Melt $1\frac{1}{2}$ bars of paraffin.

Place the relish mixture over high heat, bring to a full rolling boil, and *boil hard 1 minute,* stirring constantly. Remove from heat; *at once* stir in Certo fruit pectin. Skim off foam with metal spoon; stir and skim 5 minutes to prevent floating fruit.

While skimming the relish, remove glasses and invert to drain. Fill glasses. Cover with hot paraffin. Cool, label and store.

• Own a blender? Then try this remarkable new trophy that contains all the goodness of old-fashioned apple butter but requires none of the old-fashioned expenditure of time at the stove.

28. BLENDER SPICY APPLE JAM

5 cups prepared fruit
(about 3½ lbs.)
2 cups water
7½ cups sugar

1 teaspoon ground allspice
1½ teaspoons ground cinnamon
¼ cup lemon juice (2 lemons)
½ bottle Certo fruit pectin

Peel, cut in eighths, and core ripe apples. Place a fourth of the apples and ½ cup water in electric blender; blend at high speed about 15 seconds. Repeat 3 more times with remaining apples and water. Measure 5 cups into a large cook pot. Add sugar, spices, and lemon juice, and mix well.

Sterilize 11 8-ounce jelly glasses, wide-mouth funnel and dipper. Melt 2 bars of paraffin.

Place apple mixture over high heat, bring to a full rolling boil, and *boil hard 1 minute,* stirring constantly. Remove from heat; *at once* stir in Certo fruit pectin. Skim off foam.

Remove glasses and invert to drain. Fill glasses. Cover with hot paraffin. Cool, label and store.

• No hunter worth her gift closet can afford to ignore the bounty that's rampant in the market stalls now. Tomatoes, grapes, pears and plums are displaying their lovely colors like peacocks. Do try to capture at least one of each color in the following trophies.

The three tomato chutneys differ in appearance, though all are equally beautiful, and in taste, though all are equally delicious. They are alike in that each brings raves of delight from those fortunate enough to receive it in their gift assortment.

Your guide has donated jars of all three to church bazaars and club auctions, and has been happy to note that these exotic chutneys brought the highest prices always and were the first to be snapped up by eager buyers.

29. TOMATO-APPLE CHUTNEY

4 cups chopped tomatoes
   (about 12-13 medium)
2 cups chopped apples
   (about 1½ lbs.)
1 cup chopped green pepper
   (3 medium)
¾ cup chopped onion
   (2 or 3 medium)

⅔ cup seedless raisins
1½ cups brown sugar
½ teaspoon salt
½ teaspoon Tabasco sauce
1 teaspoon celery seed
1 cup bottled lemon juice
2 teaspoons ground ginger

Wash tomatoes; drop in boiling water for 1 minute, then into cold water. Slip off skins, and chop tomatoes coarsely. Wash, core and pare apples; chop coarsely. Wash and chop green peppers, discarding seeds and white membrane. Peel and chop onions. Measure sugar in large bowl; add salt, celery seed and ground ginger, and mix well.

Place chopped fruit and vegetables in a large cook pot. Add raisins, Tabasco, lemon juice and mixed sugar and spices. Mix well. Place over medium heat and bring to a boil. Boil, stirring occasionally, until chutney thickens, about 20 minutes.

While chutney is cooking, sterilize 6 8-ounce jars and lids, wide-mouth funnel and dipper.

When chutney is ready, remove jars and invert to drain. Fill jars to within $\frac{1}{4}$ inch of tops. Place hot jar lids on jars. Screw on bands tightly. Cool, label and store.

• This chutney is a tangy, spicy one that is marvelous with meats of all kinds, but is unsurpassed as a topping for thick hamburgers or hot dogs.

30. TOMATO-PEAR CHUTNEY

5 cups tomatoes
   (about 15 medium)
5 cups pears (about 3½ lbs.)
1 cup green pepper
   (3 medium)
1 cup chopped onions
   (4 medium)
2 cups sugar

1 cup white vinegar
2 teaspoons salt
1 teaspoon ground ginger
1 teaspoon dry mustard
$\frac{1}{4}$ teaspoon red pepper (or 1
   teaspoon Tabasco sauce)
$\frac{1}{2}$ cup canned pimento

Wash tomatoes, drop in boiling water for 1 minute, then into cold water. Slip off skins; cut each tomato into eighths. Peel, core and dice pears. Chop peppers, discarding seeds and white membrane. Peel and chop onions. Mix sugar, salt and dry spices.

Place chopped fruit and vegetables in a large cook pot. Add vinegar, sugar and spice mixture and Tabasco. Reserve chopped pimento till later. Bring chutney to a boil, stirring occasionally, and boil until thickened, about 45 minutes to 1 hour.

While boiling the chutney, sterilize 9 8-ounce jars and lids, wide-mouth funnel and dipper. When chutney has thickened, add the pimento and boil 3 minutes longer.

Remove jars from boiling water and invert to drain. Fill jars to within $\frac{1}{4}$ inch of tops. Add lids to jars. Screw bands on tightly. Cool, label and store.

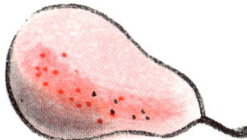

31. TOMATO-PINEAPPLE CHUTNEY

6 cups tomatoes
 (16-18 medium)
1 orange and 1 lemon
1 can crushed pineapple
 (14 oz.)
½ teaspoon salt
2 cups light brown sugar
2¼ cups white sugar
1 cup light or dark raisins
1 teaspoon ground ginger

½ teaspoon ground nutmeg
1 stick (3 inch) cinnamon
1 tablespoon mustard seed
½ teaspoon garlic powder
2 teaspoons onion powder
1 teaspoon Tabasco sauce
4 tablespoons Worcestershire
 sauce
¾ cup vinegar

Wash tomatoes; drop in boiling water 1 minute, then drop in cold water. Slip off skins; chop coarsely. Measure 6 cups; drain ¾ cup juice from tomatoes, pressing slightly if necessary. Drain juice from pineapple. Combine juices in small saucepan.

Peel ½ of yellow part of rind from both orange and lemon, and discard. Thinly slice or chop the rest of orange and lemon, and add to juices in saucepan. Cover and cook until peel is tender. If juice cooks down too much before peel is tender, add a little water or more tomato juice.

Combine in large cook pot the tomatoes, pineapple, orange and lemon mixture, sugar, salt, raisins, ginger, nutmeg and cinnamon stick.

Bring to a boil, and cook rapidly, stirring often, until tomatoes are clear and syrup is honey-thick. Takes about 45 minutes. Remove cinnamon stick. Add vinegar, mustard seed, garlic powder and onion powder, and the Tabasco and Worcestershire sauces. Boil slowly for 15 minutes more, stirring often.

While chutney is boiling, sterilize 9 8-ounce jars and lids, wide-mouth funnel and dipper.

When chutney is ready, remove jars and invert to drain. Fill to within ¼ inch of tops. Place lids on jars. Screw bands on tightly. Cool, label and store.

• Long ago, when the bright red tomato was known as the "love apple," it was thought poisonous and was grown only for its decorative beauty in the garden.

However, from the time it was found to be wholesome and delicious, it has been hunted with enthusiasm for its role in two traditional trophies. No guidebook of consequence omits directions for capturing Chili Sauce and Tomato Preserves, though each guide may differ on the paths taken.

Following are directions leading to the capture of the old-time trophies that grandmothers served with pride, and grandchildren remember with mouth-watering longing.

Another little-known trophy follows that makes use of those last small green tomatoes which are in danger of being lost due to frost if not gathered from the garden in time. If you don't grow tomatoes, take a hunting trip to find plenty of these little green critters on market stalls or country road stands in the fall. They can be captured in a delectable pickle syrup, and the results of your hunting will grace the prettiest table.

32. CHILI SAUCE

6 cups prepared tomatoes (about 16-18 medium)	1 tablespoon salt
	1½ teaspoons ground cinnamon
1 cup green peppers (4 medium)	1½ teaspoons ground cloves
	1½ teaspoons ground allspice
1 cup onions (4 medium)	1½ teaspoons nutmeg
1½ cups vinegar	1 teaspoon celery seed
1½ cups sugar	1 teaspoon mustard seed

Wash and core tomatoes. Wash green peppers and remove seeds and white membrane. Peel onions. Grind tomatoes, peppers and onions, using fine blade of grinder. Place in large cook pot, and add all the other ingredients. Mix well. Bring to a boil, and boil over medium heat for about an hour and a quarter, stirring frequently.

Sterilize 8 8-ounce jars and lids, wide-mouth funnel and dipper.

Test the chili sauce after the sauce has cooked down and thickened by placing a teaspoon of the sauce on a small plate; if no juice runs freely when the plate is tipped (after the sauce has cooled a bit) it is ready to put in the jars.

Remove the jars and invert to drain. Fill the jars. Place lids on jars. Screw bands on tightly. Cool, label and store.

33. TOMATO PRESERVES

7½ cups prepared red or yellow tomatoes	1 tart orange (navel type)
	½ teaspoon salt
6 cups light brown sugar	1 teaspoon ground ginger
1 large lemon	3 or 4 inch stick cinnamon

Wash tomatoes, drop into boiling water for 1 minute, then into cold water. Slip off skins, core and cut into two or three parts (leave yellow tomatoes whole.) Place in layers, alternating with sugar, in a large bowl. Cover bowl and leave in refrigerator for 6 or 7 hours or overnight.

Thinly pare lemon and orange peel (a vegetable peeler does best job) and use only half of each peel. Cut peel into 1 inch slivers. Remove and discard the white inner membrane or thick underpeel from the fruit. Thinly slice the peeled lemon and orange, discarding seeds, and cook along with the half-amount of peels in just enough water to prevent scorching for ten minutes. If not pre-cooked before adding to sugar, the peel is likely to be tough. Turn sugared tomatoes into large cook pot, and all other ingredients including the water used in cooking peel, and boil gently till tomatoes are clear and the syrup thick. The preserve is "right" when the syrup in a teaspoonful dropped onto a cold saucer will not run freely when the saucer is tipped.

While preserve is cooking, sterilize 6 8-ounce jars and lids, or 6 8-ounce baby-food jars, wide-mouth funnel and dipper. If using baby-food jars, melt 1 bar of paraffin.

It is not necessary to boil the clean baby-food jar lids, as the preserves will be covered with the paraffin.

When preserves are properly clear and thickened, remove cinnamon sticks and skim off foam with metal spoon. Remove jars and invert to drain. Fill jars. Place hot lids on jars. Screw bands on tightly. If using baby-food jars, cover preserves with melted paraffin. Cool, label and store.

NOTE: Just recently, I read about the happy success someone achieved by adding a half-teaspoon of nutmeg to the spices in this trophy and one thinly sliced lime plus its slivered cooked rind to the other citrus peels. This variation won more applause than the original. If you are adventurous, be the first in your circle of preserve-fanciers to win acclaim by trying this variation.

34. PICKLED GREEN TOMATOES

5 cups green tomato slices
½ cup onion slices
¼ cup light brown sugar
1 cup vinegar

1 tablespoon mixed pickling
  spices
½ teaspoon garlic powder
1½ teaspoons dill seed
⅛ teaspoon Tabasco sauce

Wash, drain and slice small green tomatoes (from 1½ to 1¾ inches across at widest point). Peel and slice onions. Spread vegetables in thin layers in bowl. Sprinkle each layer with salt (sparingly). Cover bowl and let stand 6 or 7 hours or overnight.

When ready to use, rinse slices in cold water. Taste; if too salty, rinse again. Let drain 10 or more minutes.

Put sugar and vinegar in a large cook pot and heat, stirring, until sugar dissolves. Tie spices, garlic powder and dill seed in cheesecloth and drop into the syrup. Boil five minutes. Add tomatoes and onions, cover and boil five minutes. Lower heat and let simmer five minutes more.

If it now appears that you will have too little liquid to cover slices when packaged into the jars, put more vinegar on to heat. Taste pickle, and add more seasoning if wanted. Add extra hot vinegar if needed.

Sterilize 5 8-ounce jars and lids, wide-mouth funnel and dipper.

Increase heat under pickle and let boil five more minutes. Discard spice bag. Remove jars and invert to drain. Using dipper or tongs, pack slices to within ½ inch of tops of hot jars. Add boiling hot syrup to cover pickles. Place hot lids on jars. Screw bands on tightly. Cool, label and store.

• Prepare for a pear hunt, as soon as they become plentiful, to capture the next two trophies. Your guide has chosen these from many because of their wonderful flavor, appearance and difference from the ordinary whole-canned pear. Gourmets will lift eyes heavenward at their first taste of either, because each is truly food for the gods.

I hope you were smart enough to buy an extra stone crock

when you bought those for the Brandied Fruit Melange and Belle Flower's Mincemeat. If not, get on the phone now to locate one at your hardware store, antique or junk shop, for you will surely want to present gifts of Herbed Pear Pickle at Christmas. Hunt also for a bottle of white wine vinegar and a supply of your favorite herb, and you've practically got that celestial trophy made!

The second trophy, Paradise Pear Jam, is not only one of the most colorful gifts that can be given, it is a unique blend of pears with other fruits that is perfect for a spread for toast, muffins, hot breads or scones, a topping for puddings, ice cream or cupcakes, a filling to combine with cream cheese or peanut butter in sandwiches, between layers of white, yellow, spice cake or gingerbread, in little pie-crust tarts, or baked in slits of your favorite coffee biscuit twist. It is indeed a versatile trophy that will be welcomed by any name on your gift list.

35. HERBED PEAR PICKLES

8 lbs. California Bartlett pears	*2 tablespoons your favorite dried herb*
8 cups sugar	*2 tablespoons whole cloves*
1 quart white wine vinegar	*3 two-inch sticks cinnamon*

Heat wine vinegar to boiling. Add 2 tablespoons of your favorite dried herb. (Tarragon is delightfully good. If you prefer, you may use the commercially prepared tarragon vinegar, and reduce the dried herb to 1 tablespoon, or use 1 tablespoon fresh tarragon, chopped, to be added to the pears later.) Steep the dried herb in the hot wine vinegar for 10 minutes, then strain the vinegar and reserve.

Wash, peel and core pears, and cut into eighths, or into half-inch thick slices. Scald a stone crock, one-gallon size, with boiling water, and dry. Put layers of the pear slices into the crock, covering each layer with some of the sugar, cloves, pieces of the stick cinnamon, and (if desired) a sprinkling of the fresh chopped herb or dried herb. Don't overdo the herb flavoring. If the vinegar smells strongly of the herb, omit sprinkling over the pears.

Now pour over the pear slices the hot herbed vinegar, and weigh down the fruit with crumpled aluminum foil. Let stand overnight in the covered crock.

Next day pour off the liquid. Heat it to a boil and pour again over the pears. Repeat this for 5 days. Then cover crock with clean cheesecloth and place lid on tightly. Let stand in a cool place until used. Pears will keep in the crock for a year, if you can keep from eating them all beforehand or from giving them away.

36. PARADISE PEAR JAM

$2\frac{3}{4}$ cups pears (about 2 lbs.)
  1 orange
  1 lemon
  $\frac{1}{4}$ cup chopped maraschino
    cherries

1 small can crushed pineapple
  ($8\frac{1}{2}$ oz.)
5 cups sugar
1 box Sure-Jell fruit pectin
$\frac{1}{2}$ cup finely chopped citron

Remove rinds from orange and lemon in quarters; discard half the white part of rinds. Slice rinds in slivers; chop orange and lemon coarsely, and discard seeds. Wash, peel and core pears, and grind. Grind citron. Chop cherries coarsely. Combine all the fruits, including pineapple. Measure $4\frac{1}{2}$ cups of the mixture into a large cook pot. Measure sugar; set aside. Stir Sure-Jell fruit pectin into fruit.

Sterilize 8 8-ounce jars and lids or 8 8-ounce jelly glasses, wide-mouth funnel and dipper. If using glasses, melt one bar of paraffin.

Place fruit mixture over high heat; stir until mixture comes to a hard boil. *At once* stir in sugar. Bring to a full rolling boil and *boil hard for 1 minute,* stirring constantly. Remove from heat; skim and stir for 5 minutes to cool slightly and prevent floating fruit.

While skimming, remove jars or glasses and invert to drain. Fill jars or glasses. Place hot lids on jars and screw bands on tightly. Or pour melted paraffin over jam. Cool, label and store.

• A large grape-loving clique may swear allegiance to Bacchus but his followers are out-numbered by hunters who are loyal to the flavor of unfermented grape juice, particularly in the luscious perfection of jellied trophies.

Join the majority who hunt the royal purple in all its majesty, to capture the following outstanding ones.

The Tutti-Frutti is a deliciously tart, firm jelly. Its color is red rather than purple, but not the same red as that of the Cherry or Strawberry trophy. Your guide has the word of six grandchildren that the Tutti-Frutti Jelly is the perfect sandwich mate for peanut butter or cream cheese.

The deep red of this trophy, as well as its tart flavor, goes beautifully under snowy coconut on a sponge cake and is also memorable as the ruby bands in a jelly roll.

The Spiced Grape Jelly trophy is a perfect mate for venison; however, though you are the hunter in the family you may never see a haunch of venison. No matter, this trophy is polygamous! It is also the perfect mate for all domestic red meats, rabbit, duck, goose, turkey, chicken, frogs' legs — take your choice. You may be sure it will find a happy home dinner wherever it is given. Save a jar or two for your own holiday main courses.

Hunters who have grapevines of their very own are astonished, some years, at the prolific harvest produced by these vines. If you are a lucky owner of a Concord grapevine or even a wild grape-vine, or have a friend who owns one and urges its largesse on you, you will welcome the Grape Juice Trophy. Simply and easily it can be frozen in plastic containers or canned in jars, and will furnish you with delicious vitamin-rich breakfast juice, summer coolers, winter and summer party punches, and refreshing snack-drinks anytime.

You just can't let an autumn go by without capturing at least one of these grape trophies, and you'll find your gift shelf for autumn has gained added beauty.

37. TUTTI-FRUTTI JELLY

1 lb. apples (for 1 cup juice)
3½ lbs. Concord grapes
    (5 cups juice)
    (wild grapes — 5 lbs. for
    5 cups juice)

1 cup canned pineapple juice
3 tablespoons lemon juice
9 cups sugar
1½ boxes Sure-Jell fruit pectin

Wash, stem and crush grapes (may be crushed, 2 cups at a time, in a heavy plastic bag to prevent splashes). Place crushed grapes in a large cook pot, add 1½ cups water and simmer, covered, for 10 minutes.

Wash and slice apples; do not pare or core. Add ¾ cups water and simmer, covered, for 10 minutes. Crush with masher or heavy cup and simmer for 5 minutes more.

Place four thicknesses of dampened cheesecloth over a colander set in a bowl, pour grapes and apples carefully into cloth. Alternately press and squeeze out juice. Strain 1 cup pineapple juice.

Sterilize 12 8-ounce jelly glasses or 8-ounce baby-food jars, and small-mouth funnel. Melt two bars of paraffin.

Measure sugar into a large bowl. Measure 6 cups combined apple and grape juice into a large cook pot; add the strained pineapple juice and lemon juice. Mix Sure-Jell fruit pectin with juice. Stir over high heat till mixture boils hard. When juice boils hard, *at once* stir in the sugar. Return to boil, stirring often.

While jelly returns to a boil, remove glasses and invert to drain. When juice returns to a full rolling boil, *boil hard for 1 minute,* stirring constantly. Remove from heat, skim off foam with a metal spoon, and fill hot glasses. Cover jelly at once with melted paraffin. Cool, label and store.

38. SPICED GRAPE JELLY

3 lbs. ripe grapes
$\frac{1}{2}$ cup cider vinegar
1 teaspoon ground cloves

2 teaspoons ground
    cinnamon
7 cups sugar
$\frac{1}{2}$ bottle Certo fruit pectin

Stem and crush grapes (may be crushed in a heavy plastic bag to prevent splashes); add vinegar and spices. Bring to a boil in a large cook pot and simmer, covered, 10 minutes.

Place four thicknesses of cheesecloth over a colander set in a large bowl. Carefully pour grapes into cloth, and alternately press and squeeze out juice. Measure 4 cups juice into large cook pot. Add sugar to juice and mix well.

Sterilize 9 8-ounce jelly glasses or baby-food jars. Melt 2 bars of paraffin.

Place jelly mixture over high heat and bring to a boil, stirring constantly. When it boils, *at once* stir in Certo fruit pectin. Bring to a full rolling boil and *boil hard 1 minute,* stirring constantly.

Remove from heat, skim off foam with a metal spoon, and pour or ladle quickly into hot glasses. Cover at once with melted paraffin. Cool, label and store.

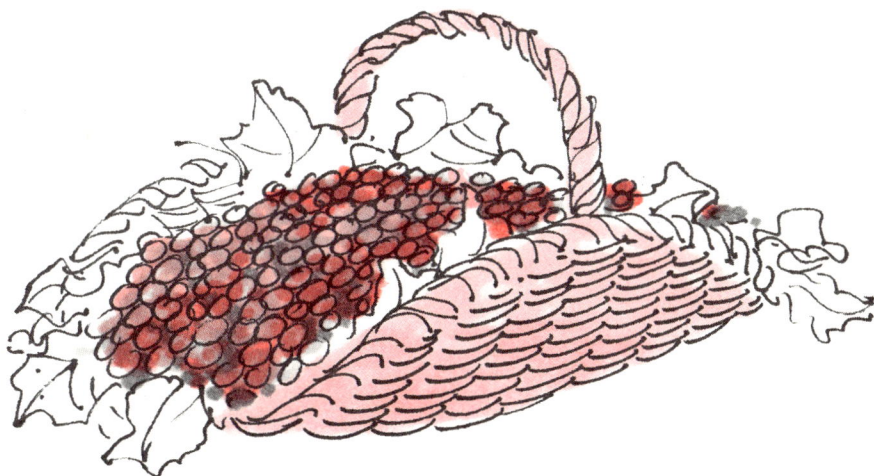

39. FROZEN OR CANNED GRAPE JUICE

12 lbs. grapes (ripe Concord) to make 16 cups juice
1 quart water   1 lb. sugar

Wash, stem and crush grapes (may be crushed, a pound or two at a time, in a heavy plastic bag to prevent splashes); place in a large cook pot over medium heat and simmer, 10 minutes, covered. Pour a quarter amount at a time into four thicknesses of cheese-cloth spread over a colander set in a large bowl. Squeeze and press out juice.

Measure 16 cups (1 gallon) juice into a very large cook pot (at least 8 quart size); add the quart of water and the pound of sugar. If you like your grape juice sweeter, you may increase the sugar to $2\frac{1}{2}$ cups.

TO CAN:

Sterilize 11 8-ounce canning jars and lids. Keep hot.

Bring the grape juice to a boil, stirring constantly. As soon as it reaches a full rolling boil, remove from heat, skim off foam if necessary with a metal spoon, and pour immediately into the hot jars. Wipe any spills from rims of jars with a clean wadded paper towel dipped in boiling water. Using tongs, place hot lids on jars. Holding each jar with oven mitt or clean tea towel, screw bands on tightly. Cool, label and store.

Remember, each jar should "click" loudly when cooling, and lids should not bulge. If any lid does not click or appears convex in shape, remove band and lid, reheat juice and use a new hot lid to reseal.

TO FREEZE:

To freeze, simply pour hot juice into plastic pint containers, add lids (allow $\frac{1}{2}$ inch space at tops of containers), cool and place in freezer.

• That well-known hunter, Little Jack Horner, thought he had captured a fine trophy when he found a plum in his Christmas pie. Evidently he knew nothing of the finer, tastier trophies made with this delectable stone-fruit. Following are hunting directions for bringing down four unusual plum trophies.

Trophy #40 is a superb Italian plum catsup that teams up with meats, breakfast toast and sausages, and toasted cheese sandwiches for luncheon or supper.

The Plum Nutty is a rich purple jam, wonderful as a spread for graham crackers and saltines, and doubles as a filling for fruit buns, coffee-cake rings and little pie-tarts.

Tiny damson plums blend with orange and walnut for a completely new taste sensation. This one is not only a conserve of beauty but a joy for the palate of any gourmet on your gift list.

Less well known but available for a short season in the Supermart Woods and on country stands is the greengage plum. If you are a lucky hunter in finding a supply of these marvelous green-gold beauties, you will be able to capture the most unusual, delicious, easiest-made trophy of all — no cooking, no crushing, no pitting or peeling, honest! Just turn to Trophy #43 for confirmation of this claim, dash off to your liquor store for a quart of good cognac and bring down your basket of greengages. In a half-hour you'll be out of the kitchen with your trophy safely captured. It's plum' amazing.

40. PRUNE-PLUM CATSUP

5 lbs. ripe purple Italian plums	1 teaspoon pepper
	1 teaspoon dry mustard
1 cup water	½ teaspoon garlic powder
1 teaspoon salt	(or 1 clove of garlic)
1 teaspoon cinnamon	4 cups sugar
1 teaspoon ground cloves	1½ cups cider vinegar
¼ teaspoon nutmeg	

Wash plums, pit them and place in a large cook pot with the cup of water. Bring to a boil, reduce heat and simmer for about 30 minutes, or until plums are mushy. Put through sieve or food mill, or if you have a blender simply blend the plums to a puree instead of using a sieve. Be careful not to put too much plum mixture into blender at one time. The blended puree will be a darker purple because all the skins are blended, also. When using the blended puree, add ⅛ teaspoon more of EACH of the spices plus ¼ cup more sugar and ⅛ cup more vinegar. Mix sugar with salt and spices and combine with plum mixture in a large cook pot; add vinegar and mix well. Bring to a boil, stirring constantly. Reduce heat and simmer 30 minutes, stirring frequently.

While catsup is simmering, sterilize 10 8-ounce jars (or baby-food jars), wide-mouth funnel, dipper and lids. If using baby-food jars, melt two bars of paraffin.

When catsup thickens, test by dropping a little in a cold saucer; if no thin liquid seeps out around the edges of the catsup, it is ready to be put into the hot jars. If you have used a garlic clove instead of garlic powder, remove it from the pot after 25 minutes of cooking.

Remove jars and invert to drain.

Ladle the catsup into the hot jars. If using baby-food jars, fill to bend of the neck of the jar. Seal with paraffin. Place lids on jars. Screw bands on tightly. Cool, label and store.

41. PLUM NUTTY

2½ lbs. ripe plums
½ cup orange juice
1½ teaspoons grated orange
    rind (optional)

½ cup walnuts
  (finely chopped)
6 cups sugar
1 box Sure-Jell fruit pectin

Wash and pit (do not peel) fully ripe plums. Cut and chop very fine. Measure 4 cups into a very large cook pot; add orange juice and grated rind and the finely chopped nuts. Mix well. Measure sugar and set aside. Add Sure-Jell fruit pectin to fruit mixture and mix well.

Sterilize 9 8-ounce jelly glasses, wide-mouth funnel and dipper. Melt two bars of paraffin.

Place fruit mixture over high heat and stir till mixture comes to a hard boil. *At once* stir in sugar. Bring to a full rolling boil and *boil hard for 1 minute,* stirring constantly. Remove from heat and skim off foam with metal spoon. Stir and skim for 5 minutes to cool slightly and prevent floating fruit.

While skimming, remove glasses from hot water and invert to drain. When ready, fill the hot glasses with the Plum Nutty. Cover at once with hot paraffin. Cool, label and store.

42. DAMSON-ORANGE CONSERVE

2 lbs. ripe damson plums
1 orange
2 cups water
½ cup seedless raisins

½ cup coarsely chopped
    walnuts
7 cups sugar
1 box Sure-Jell fruit pectin

Wash and chop the orange and rind very fine, discarding seeds. Add water and simmer in a small saucepan, covered, about 20 minutes. Pit (do not peel) and halve damsons; chop fine. Combine fruits; measure 4½ cups into a very large cook pot. Add raisins and walnuts. Measure sugar; set aside. Mix Sure-Jell fruit pectin into fruit.

Sterilize 10 8-ounce jelly glasses. Melt two bars of paraffin.

Bring conserve mixture to a hard boil over high heat, stirring constantly. *At once* stir in sugar. Bring to a full rolling boil and *boil hard 1 minute,* stirring constantly. Remove from heat; skim off foam with metal spoon. Stir and skim 5 minutes to prevent floating fruit.

While skimming, invert the hot glasses to drain. When ready, fill the hot glasses with conserve. Cover conserve with melted paraffin. Cool, label and store.

43. CHRISTMAS PLUMS

4 quarts greengage plums   *cognac*
2 cups sugar

Choose firm, ripe, perfect plums. Wash and drain thoroughly. Measure sugar into a bowl. Open a fifth or quart of good cognac.

Wash four pint canning jars; cover with boiling water in a large cook pot. Sterilize for five minutes. Drain on a tray covered with paper towels. Cover four canning lids with 1 inch boiling water in a shallow pan. Keep hot for at least two minutes.

Pack the plums carefully into the sterilized jars with alternate layers of sugar, using $\frac{1}{2}$ cup sugar to each jar. Fill jars to within 1 inch of tops. Pour in cognac till filled. Place hot lids on jars, and screw bands on tightly. Store in a cool dark place for about 1 month before using. Turn jars upside down each week for about ten minutes. Be sure to label the jars if you are giving these luscious plums as gifts.

• At this point the plethora of shining jewel-hued trophies on your shelves may tempt you to sample this or splurge with that, especially when having dinner guests.

Before you succumb, remember that while you can buy another bottle or tin or bird, you can't replace trophies containing spring strawberries, summer cantaloupe and such till next year. Resist temptation unless you're sure you'll have enough of them remaining to fill your gift list needs.

Chapter V

Winter's Hounds are on the Traces
More Relishes and Chutneys

Thanksgiving's date creeps closer and the hunting season is on the wane. For those who were smart marksmen in acquiring that crock of Belle Flower's Mincemeat around the middle of October (and have added the extra cider and sherry after the two weeks' ripening) now is the time to put it into jars as directed. Sneak out one quart for your Thanksgiving pie and an extra cup for Trophy #44, Orange-Pumpkin Conserve.

Remember that pumpkin you were advised to bring down at the beginning of Chapter IV? The cheerful globe that has brightened your kitchen shelf or dinner table centerpiece can now be put to its second use as the main ingredient in this trophy. What a delicious concoction it is, to be served with turkey, chicken or other birds, or ham, as a filling for little pie-crust turnovers, and as a topping for hot biscuits or muffins!

And if your pumpkin is a large one, six pounds or more, you should have enough diced pumpkin left to capture also Trophy #45, a luscious pickle that teams up with any meat course.

44. ORANGE-PUMPKIN CONSERVE

2 large Florida oranges	5 cups sugar
1 cup orange juice	1 teaspoon cinnamon
2 quarts finely diced pumpkin	1 cup mincemeat
½ teaspoon salt	1 cup pecan halves

Wash pumpkin, cut into quarters for easier handling, and peel thinly, discarding rind, seeds and stringy membrane. Dice into very small cubes or pieces.

Wash oranges, cut into small pieces including rind, and discard seeds. Combine oranges, orange juice, pumpkin and salt in a large cook pot. Cook until pumpkin is tender (15-20 minutes), then add sugar, spices and mincemeat. If mixture seems a bit low on liquid at this point, add about ¼ cup more orange juice. Simmer over a low flame until mixture is thick and glossy, stirring frequently. This should take about 25 minutes.

While mixture is simmering, sterilize 8 8-ounce jars, lids, wide-mouth funnel and dipper.

Add pecans to mixture for the last five minutes of cooking time.

Remove jars from boiling water and invert to drain. When conserve is ready, fill jars to ½ inch from top. Seal with hot lids and bands, screwing bands on tightly. Cool, label and store.

45. PICKLED ORANGE-PUMPKIN

2½ cups sugar	1 pint cider vinegar
2 two-inch pieces stick cinnamon	1½ cups water
½ teaspoon ground allspice	2 quarts diced pumpkin (3 lbs.)
¾ teaspoon whole cloves	½ can (3 oz.) frozen orange juice, undiluted
½ teaspoon ground ginger	

Wash pumpkin, cut into quarters for easier handling, and peel thinly, discarding rind, seeds and stringy membrane. Dice into one-inch cubes. Measure two quarts or eight cups.

Combine sugar, spices, vinegar and water in a large cook pot. Bring to boil, and boil till sugar dissolves.

Add pumpkin and orange juice concentrate, and return to boil. Reduce heat; simmer until cubes become tender (about 30 minutes).

While pickle is simmering, sterilize 7 8-ounce jars, lids, wide-mouth funnel and dipper. Drain inverted jars just before pickle is ready. Fill hot jars to ½ inch of tops. Seal with hot lids, and screw bands on tightly. Cool, label and store.

• Now, before the first Christmas horn blows, the hunter's horn catches the last little empty jars lurking sneakily in the basement gloom or the apartment cupboard. If you've missed out on a season and your shelves have large gaps like missing teeth, you can still make an impression with a couple of the seven fillers that follow. These marvelously easy trophies can be captured at *any time,* since they call for only canned, dried, bottled or frozen ingredients. They can actually be the first trophies to be bagged during the quiet months of February and March for the following Christmas, giving you the jump on your hunting seasons next year. A quick trip to the supermart or food market will fill all your ammunition needs for any of these unusual fillers.

No holiday dinner is complete without that extra touch of unusual "company" luxury. A jar of Gourmet Chutney is not only something different to complement the festive bird, but it makes a gift which will endow the giver with a Class A Chef's reputation.

Trophy #48, Corn Relish, is easy to capture, yet it looks and tastes like a terrific accomplishment by the hunter-giver. Don't be discouraged by the variety of ingredients; if you check each item you'll find you already have most of them on hand. This trophy is a rich golden jewel that sets off the darker colors of the conserves and jellies in gift baskets. A spoonful turns a peasant hamburger into a royal dish.

Apricot-Ginger Jam is unusual because it calls for crystallized ginger, which can be purchased in any good candy shop or candy counter in a department store. A delicious treat in itself, it adds that gourmet touch to this easiest-of-all-to-make winter jam.

Canned-Peach Chili Sauce is a peachy delicious delight to the taste buds (especially when combined with roast beef or ham) and it smells better than any perfume while it is simmering. You may look like the wrath of Diana while hunting, but men will grow dreamy-eyed and interested when approaching your aromatic door.

Chutneys usually are associated with curry dishes, but Trophy #51, Cranberry Chutney, goes equally well with turkey, ham, all other birds, and even stews and sausage meat. It tastes as delicious in summer as at Christmas.

For a fast, last-minute trophy (in case you've forgotten a name or two until that last horn blows) nothing is so easy or quick to capture as this superb Wine Jelly Trophy. It's especially appropriate to give that bachelor who throws slick cocktail parties with way-out canapes, or to the hostess who seems to have everything. Little jewelled drops of this jelly pretty up little crackers spread first with cheese, ham spread, peanut butter even, — in fact, any kind of spread except the seafood ones.

You may take the word of your guide that these wonderful last-minute fillers are so easy and quick to capture that you can bring down two of them in a single day. Even in the rush of holiday preparations there is always a spare hour or two to go hunting and the results in your gift closet will repay you many times over with the appreciation and pleasure expressed by those who receive and enjoy your gifts.

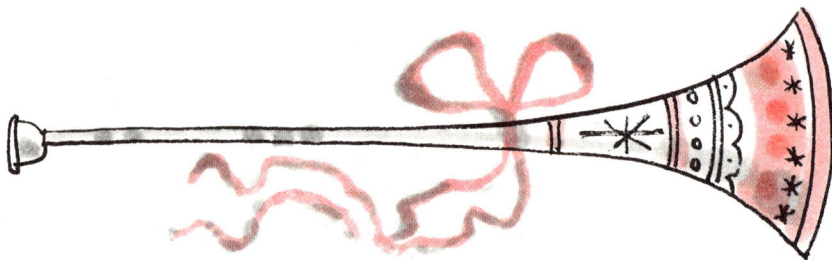

46. GOURMET CHUTNEY

2 cans (1 lb. 14 oz.)
    crushed pineapple
2 cups cider vinegar
2 cups brown sugar
1 teaspoon salt
1 cup slivered almonds

1 cup seedless raisins
1 chopped green pepper
1 teaspoon ground ginger
½ teaspoon garlic powder
    (or 2 crushed garlic
    cloves)

Place pineapple, vinegar, brown sugar and salt in large cook pot. Bring to boil and cook slowly, stirring frequently, for 25 minutes.

While cooking mixture, sterilize 8 8-ounce jars, lids, wide-mouth funnel and dipper.

After mixture has cooked for 25 minutes, add garlic, nuts, raisins, seeded green pepper and ginger. Cook slowly till thickened, stirring often.

When mixture has thickened, invert jars to drain. Fill jars to within ½ inch of tops. Place lids on jars; add bands and screw on tightly. Cool, label and store.

47. CARROT MARMALADE

2 lbs. carrots
2 oranges
4 lemons
7 cups sugar

½ bottle Certo fruit pectin
    (optional) 2 teaspoons
    ground ginger or
    cinnamon

Wash, scrape or peel carrots; cook about 15 minutes or until tender.

Wash oranges, grate rind and dice pulp of oranges, discarding any seeds. Squeeze juice from lemons. Drain carrots, chop very fine, and mix with orange pulp, rind and lemon juice. Measure 4 cups of mixture into a large cook pot. Mix sugar with fruit. If adding spice, mix it with the sugar before blending with fruit.

Sterilize 10 8-ounce jelly glasses, wide-mouth funnel and dipper. Melt 2 bars of paraffin.

71

Bring carrot mixture to a boil over high heat, stirring constantly. When mixture reaches a full rolling boil, *boil hard 1 minute,* stirring constantly. Remove from heat; *at once* stir in Certo fruit pectin. Skim off foam with metal spoon. Stir and skim 5 minutes to cool slightly and prevent floating fruit.

While skimming, remove glasses from hot water, invert to drain, and ladle marmalade into the hot glasses. Cover with hot paraffin. Cool, label and store.

48. CANNED CORN RELISH

3 (12 oz.) cans whole kernel
    corn
1 cup chopped onion
1 cup thin-sliced celery
½ cup chopped green pepper
1 can (4 oz.) drained diced
    pimento
1 cup sugar
1 tablespoon salt
1 teaspoon Tabasco sauce
    (optional)

½ teaspoon garlic powder
    (not garlic salt)
1 tablespoon mustard seed
1 tablespoon celery seed
½ teaspoon ground ginger
3 cups white vinegar
    (divided)
1½ tablespoons dry mustard
1 teaspoon turmeric
¼ cup flour
¼ cup corn liquid from can

Drain corn, reserving ¼ cup liquid. Peel and chop onion; remove seeds and chop green pepper; thinly slice celery; dice pimento. Combine onion, celery, green pepper, pimento, sugar, salt, Tabasco, garlic powder, celery seeds and mustard seeds, ginger and 2½ cups vinegar in a large cook pot, and bring to a boil. Boil 5 minutes, stirring occasionally. Blend mustard, turmeric and flour with corn liquid until smooth, and thin with remaining ½ cup vinegar. Add to hot mixture and cook 5 or 6 minutes till liquid thickens, stirring occasionally.

While cooking mixture, sterilize 8 8-ounce jars, lids, wide-mouth funnel and dipper.

When relish liquid thickens to a creamy consistency, add the corn. Boil 5 minutes longer. While it is boiling, remove jars from hot water and invert to drain.

When relish is ready, ladle into hot jars. Add hot lids, and seal with bands, screwing bands on tightly. Cool, label and store.

49. APRICOT-GINGER JAM

1 lb. box dried apricots*
1 can (1 lb. 4 oz.) crushed
    pineapple
3½ cups sugar
2½ cups water

½ teaspoon salt
2 medium diced, peeled
    oranges
4 oz. crystallized ginger

Remove peel and seeds from oranges and discard. Dice pulp of oranges and chop ginger into small bits. Mix all ingredients together in a large cook pot, and boil until there is only a little free liquid when a spoonful of the mixture is placed on a cold saucer.

While boiling and stirring the jam, sterilize 6 8-ounce jars, lids, wide-mouth funnel and dipper. When jam thickens, remove jars and invert to drain.

Fill jars to ⅛ inch of tops. Add lids. Screw bands on tightly. Cool, label and store.

*Be sure to check weight of box. You must have 16 ounces of dried fruit.

50. CANNED PEACH CHILI SAUCE

7 cups sliced canned peaches (about 2 large and 1 medium sized
   cans)

1 large green pepper	½ cup sugar
1 large onion	3 teaspoons salt
½ cup syrup from peaches	3 teaspoons cinnamon
1½ cups vinegar	1 teaspoon ground cloves
½ teaspoon celery seed	½ teaspoon ground allspice

Drain peaches thoroughly. Remove seeds and white membrane
from pepper and peel onion. Put peaches, pepper and onion
through food chopper, using medium knife (or chop finely with
sharp knife). Combine with remaining ingredients and simmer
about 1 hour, stirring frequently.

About fifteen minutes before chili is finished, sterilize 5 8-ounce
jars or baby-food jars, wide-mouth funnel, dipper and lids. If using
baby-food jars, melt bar of paraffin.

When chili sauce has thickened (when almost no free liquid
runs from a spoonful placed on a cold saucer) remove jars and
invert to drain. Fill drained hot jars to within ¼ inch of tops.
Add hot lids, and screw bands on tightly. If using baby-food jars,
seal with melted paraffin. Cool, label and store.

51. CRANBERRY CHUTNEY

1½ lbs. (1½ cans) whole
    cranberry sauce
1½ cups vinegar
1½ cups brown sugar
¾ cup seedless raisins
¾ cup blanched almonds,
    chopped finely

1 teaspoon garlic salt
1 teaspoon ground ginger
¼ teaspoon nutmeg
¼ teaspoon red pepper
    or ¼ teaspoon Tabasco
    sauce

Combine all ingredients in a large cook pot, mix thoroughly and bring to a boil. Boil slowly, stirring occasionally, until the chutney is fairly thick, or when almost no free liquid runs from a spoonful dropped on a cold saucer.

When chutney is partially thickened (or after about twenty minutes of cooking time), sterilize 6 or 7 8-ounce jars, lids, wide-mouth funnel and dipper.

When chutney is ready, remove jars and invert to drain. Ladle chutney into jars. Add hot lids, and screw bands on tightly. Cool, label and store.

52. WINE JELLY

    2 cups good wine (sherry or muscatel for a golden jelly, port or
        cherry wine for a royal ruby, Concord grape wine for a
        glowing purple)
    3 cups sugar   ½ bottle Certo fruit pectin

Pour wine into double boiler top, and mix in sugar. Cook over boiling water for a few minutes until wine is very hot.

While heating wine, sterilize 4 8-ounce jelly glasses or baby-food jars, small-mouth funnel and tongs. Melt ½ bar of paraffin. Remove glasses and invert to drain.

Stir wine thoroughly, making sure all liquid is heated thoroughly. Then mix all the liquid pectin at once into the hot wine. Stir thoroughly, remove from fire and pour into the hot drained glasses or jars. Seal with melted paraffin. Cool, label and store.

Chapter VI

Home is the Hunter

Packaging your Trophies

Now is the time for all good hunters to take a happy inventory of their game bags. I hope you remembered to keep that tally of each trophy brought down during the year, and deducted any that were eaten or given away.

Total up the number of jars on the list. On another sheet of paper, jot down the names of those lucky enough to rate a Christmas gift from you, leaving a space between each name. In this space write the titles of the jars each will receive. For example:

Aunt Gatrooda:

> Cherry Jelly, Peach-Cantaloupe Conserve, Tomato Preserves, Corn Relish

Zeke:

> Strawberry Preserves, Cucumber Crisps, Tomato-Pear Chutney, Apricot-Ginger Jam

Try to choose assortments for each person that are varied in color, consistency and type. But at the same time take into account Aunt Gatrooda's possible allergies, Zeke's preference for sweets, etc. In other words, show by your gift assortment that you *care* about the recipient; this thoughtfulness is the difference that makes your gift remembered with real appreciation.

 76

As you write each title, check it off your tally sheet so you will know at a glance just how many of each kind are left. This is important because around Christmastime you'll be feeling so successful and relaxed that before you've completed your Christmas list, you'll give in to impulse giving — to neighbors, the mailman, your dentist or even completely unknown indigents who happen to knock at your door. A few of these impulses left unmarked on your tally sheet can leave you minus some special jar earmarked for a particular friend.

The number of trophies given to each recipient will depend on the total you have bagged and retained, of course, but if you were a persevering marksman during the year, you should be able to be pretty extravagant!

When you are ready to package your gifts, remove one person's allotment at a time. Wrap and label it before going on to the next, otherwise you may become all out at the eyes from the different sparkling colors and wind up mistakenly tagging those exotic chutneys and relishes slated for Bob the Bachelor to jelly-loving, toothless Aunt Woozie.

Now for a word on gift-wrapping your booty-turned-bounty. My suggestions are based on the fact that your trophies are already as lovely as lilies and need no gilding. But they must be packaged to protect their fragility and to render them transportable, and this may be accomplished in attractive and inexpensive ways.

Some suggested items to acquire for packaging are:
Clear cellophane tape
Seals of assorted sizes
Tissue wrap
Green or white "Easter" grass
Rolls of cellophane sheets in any preferred color
Gift-wrap or foil
Ribbons, and gold or silver cord
Heavy cardboard, preferrably corrugated type
Nylon net in bright colors

77

Containers (sized according to number of jars per gift):
    Deep bread or roll baskets of reed or plastic
    Shoeboxes (covered with gift wrap or foil)
    Large plastic containers (freezer or refrigerator bowls)
    Easter baskets (spray with gold or silver paint)
    Little plastic trays (the kind in which tomatoes are marketed)
    Larger plastic trays (the kind in which mushrooms are
        marketed)
    Heavy foil bags
    Fancy fifth-sized or quart-sized whiskey cartons
    Lifoam containers (ice buckets, hot roll baskets, or six-pak
        beer coolers)
    Styrofoam trays (these come indented, packed with new jelly
        glasses)

If you are giving more than four jars as one gift, you will probably use bread or roll baskets, covered shoeboxes, plastic or Lifoam containers or trays, or gilded Easter baskets. Line chosen container with either crumpled tissue wrap or Easter grass. Press jars into tissue or grass so they will not tip over easily. Press more tissue or grass between each jar to protect the glass walls of each from its neighbor. Center a Chistmas seal of appropriate size on top of each jar lid, and since gummed seals have a tendency to pop off glass or metal surfaces after drying out, take the precaution of reinforcing each seal with tiny slivers of cellophane tape. Wrap the gift in a sheet of colored cellophane and tie with contrasting or matching ribbons. If the container is round in shape, the ribbon may slip so anchor it here and there with cellophane tape. Attach a sprig of holly and a gift tag — and lo, you have not a gilded lily but a most appropriate and very pretty Christmas package.

Three or four baby-food jars fit beautifully in those plastic tomato trays (which I hope you remembered to save during the year as I suggested way back). Cut a piece of heavy cardboard to fit the bottom of a tray. Cover the cardboard with gift wrap, tissue or foil. Place in the tray. Cut a strip of cellophane tape as long as the tray and place it, sticky side up, on the cardboard. Set each jar down firmly on the tape, leaving a small space between each jar. Press crumpled strips of tissue between each jar to protect sides against breakage.

Center Christmas seals of appropriate size on top of each jar lid, reinforcing seals with tiny strips of cellophane tape. Turn a second tray upside down over the tops of the jars, then tie trays together with ribbon or cord at each end and in the middle. Wrap in cellophane, foil or gift wrap, tie with ribbon, and attach a sprig of holly and a gift tag. Result: a package that is a conversation piece!

A large jar of mincemeat can be packaged, well padded with tissue, in a foil gift bag. Cut a piece of heavy cardboard to fit the bottom of the bag, or gift wrap a package of piecrust mix and place it in the bottom. This prevents the bag from tipping over and helps protect the bottom of the jar. Press Easter grass or crumpled tissue wrap tightly around the sides of the jar, filling the bag as much as possible. Tie top of bag with gold or silver cord, add a small red poinsettia and gift tag, and voilà! A package fit for a king or queen.

In an emergency, when I've run out of containers and have an expectant but unexpected giftee waiting at the door, I've made good use of those fancy cardboard containers in which fifths or quarts of spirits make their appearance around the holidays. I slip in the three or four small jars of goodies well protected with tissue padding between each, reseal the top of the container with a large gummed seal, add gift tag and a fat ribbon bow on top, and sit back for the compliments on an unusual package.

Among the packaging items listed, note the inclusion of nylon net. This inexpensive material is sheer magic! Its delicate appearance masks an ability to withstand crushing, and when made into fluffy "poms" leads a double life, first as a lovely gift package accent and later as a groovy pot-scrubber that lasts from one Christmas to the next. It is tough enough to clean metal pots and pans yet will not mar the finest enamel on cookware or fingernails.

Nylon net can be found in thirty-six inch width, doubled, at yard-goods counters in department stores. Yard lengths in three colors will produce from eighteen large to twenty-seven medium pot-scrubber poms at a cost of about two dollars.

To make the poms, cut each doubled yard piece into either nine equal doubled strips, four inches wide for medium-sized poms, or into six equal doubled strips, six inches wide for large-sized poms. Thread a large-eyed needle with heavy thread of matching or con-trasting color; knot the two ends together. Beginning at one end of a doubled strip of net, anchor the thread to the net leaving enough thread at the knotted end to tie to, later. Stitch a line of large (about 1/4 inch) running stitches along the center of the strip lengthwise, to the opposite end.

Then, wrapping the knotted end around your finger, push and pull the net together, drawing the thread up tightly so that the net puckers into a butterfly shape.

Fasten securely by wrapping extra thread around the middle of the butterfly a few times and then pushing the needle and thread back and forth through the middle. Tie knotted end and needle end of thread in a tight knot. Leaving about four inches of thread attached for fastening to gift, cut off needle. Twist and pull the edge of each layer of net into a ruffled appearance until the whole forms an airy "pouf" ball, a pretty practical pot-scrubber pom, an additional bonus with any gift package. Be sure to tell your recipients about the pom's usefulness lest it wind up with discarded gift wrap due to his ignorance of the finer things in pot scrubbing.

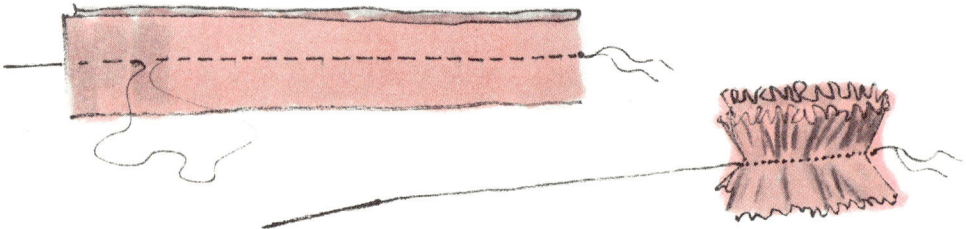

TAKE THE WRAP WITHOUT A YAP

Others' gifts are wrapped with care,
Their satin bows tied with a flair,
Their covers minus rip or tear
Or wrinkle ever.

Others manage loops and swirls,
Small bows, large bows, fancy furls,
Rosettes, pompons, even curls
With slight endeavor.

Others' wrappings never split
Around box corners, not a bit;
Their foil is always cut to fit.
O happy sever!

We cut and fit and fold and tie
Each package with great do-or-die.
The finished product makes us sigh,
We're just not clever.

We comfort us with this bromide:
The *thought's* what counts, not what's outside
Nor even what might be inside —
Well-l-l, almost never!

Chapter VII

Fresh Triumphs in the Field

What to buy

Even though your gift cupboard contains many trophies gathered from the foregoing section, you may want to augment your reputation as a star gift-giver by going on a short safari in pursuit of additional dainties. Or, if you are a latecomer and haven't gone hunting through the year, join us now.

The title of this chapter refers to the condition of those little delicacies, the Christmas cookies, in their state of perfection. Caught on the wing, figuratively speaking.

Although there is no bag-limit on these tiny critters, the open season is short unless you own a freezer and can take advantage of the fact that cookies *can* be brought down and frozen ahead

 82

of time. To catch enough of them is easy, however, and to trap their pristine freshness for any length of time is also easy if you know the few basic rules of preservation practiced by the experts who indulge in this sport for the purpose of gift-giving.

If I am accepted as guide, I will provide you with opportunities to snare as many of these wee beauties in varied shapes, colors and flavors as you choose. Don't worry about a thing; I will lead you safely past the potholes of poor judgment, the pitfalls of soggy and stale, and the tentacles of the too-little and/or too-late. You will be spared the horrors of the unwanted gift or the empty hand at gift-time because I promise to deliver you, victorious and loaded (with game, that is) in time to relax and enjoy your holidays. If you need more persuasion, go back and read page 7 again. The remarks therein apply to this section as well.

Now that you've been persuaded to go hunting, let's get your equipment together. Assuming you have never gone on a Christmas Cookie Safari, you may be lacking certain essentials. Here is a list of them, all inexpensive and all available at housewares sections in department stores, five-and-dime stores or supermarts.

Cookie sheets (preferably four)
Cookie cutters in Christmas designs
Measuring spoons
Measuring cups (dry and wet measure)
Rolling pin
Pancake turner
Flour-sifter
Cookie press

For cooling, packing and storing the little critters:
Paper towels
Plastic freezer bags or Saran Wrap
Easter grass
Cans with tight lids
(large, for storing, smaller for gifts)

Optional, but time and labor savers, are the electric mixer and blender.

Four cookie sheets may sound like too many, but you'll discover how much time this number will save; for example, two sheets of cookies in the oven while you prepare two more, or two sheets of cookies cooling while two are baking, or (if you have a double-rack large oven) one whole batch of tiny cookies fitting on four sheets at once thereby saving several periods of baking time.

Variety is the spice of a can of gift cookies so you will want to make at least two kinds of drop cookies, one rolled and cut-out cookie type, and two or more kinds shaped by the cookie press.

A pancake turner is useful in removing the cookies from the sheets, especially the more delicate varieties.

It isn't really necessary to cool cookies on a wire rack. If you haven't a rack, spread several paper towels over thick newspapers on a sofa, bed or even ironing board in a room away from the kitchen; any of these will serve as a cooling table and save needed counter or table space in the kitchen while baking is going on.

When you've been on a few of these yearly hunting trips, you'll find yourself becoming a collector of cans. Every cookie caught on this book's safari is a *crisp* critter which keeps best in cans with *tight* lids. I do not advise keeping cookies in cardboard boxes, cookie jars with loose lids, stone crocks or any fancy but unsuitable containers *unless* such containers are lined with either airtight sheets of plastic wrap large enough to be folded over several times on top of the cookies or unless the cookies are placed in plastic freezer bags which are then closed at the top with tape or rubber bands; all air and humidity must be kept from attacking the freshness of the cookies. The soft cookie, the chewy cookie and their ilk are not included in this collection because they cannot be packed with crisp ones without imparting some of their moisture to the crisp ones. This moisture will ruin the crispness and lessen the keeping qualities of all.

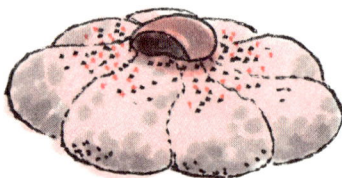

It becomes easy to acquire cans with lids after awhile. Once your friends and relatives are gifted with your luscious largesse, they become can savers for you. Some will gleefully produce *bigger* cans than they received from you last year, hoping for the bigger ones' return filled to the brim. You will be presented with nut cans, coffee cans, candy cans, fruit cake tins, larger than fruit cake tins — in fact, you will be forced to cry "Can it!" when your prowess as a cookie-giver spreads around and you find yourself up to your ears in cans by February.

One last comment before taking off on our hunt. If you find time to paint and decorate your gift cans (see the last part of this chapter for tips on simple decorating) you won't get many of *them* returned if your experience parallels mine. This decorated can disappearance puzzles me. Is it a compliment to my artistic ability? Are they being used for other cookies, potato chips, screws and nails or hoarded string? Perhaps children are given these cans to play kick-the-can, or the trashmobile's monstrous press flattens them. This puzzle is something I mull over when I am not out hunting.

If you would like to try your hand at fancying up your cans, here is a step-by-step method. Actually, you can do this anytime of year except possibly the last two weeks of December. You'll be spending a good share of those two weeks bringing down the little fillers.

If your cans are printed all over with advertising blurb and the names of the original product in garish colors, a ground coat of flat paint is called for. You can use up any old leftover paint around the house because the top coat of enamel which follows will cover it. But don't try to skip this ground coat for enamel alone won't cover a brilliant orange and blue combination, black letters or even brown and yellow.

Let the ground coat dry overnight. Then apply your enamel. Don't forget the lids, also, unless they are plastic "snap-on" lids. Christmas decals from the five-and-dime store may be applied to these lids but not paint. Don't paint the insides of cans either, for the paint odor may linger to spoil the delicate taste of your cookies.

Let the enamel dry for two days. Next, using a child's paintbrush and gold or silver paint, write the word COOKIES on one side of each can in your neatest script or print. Then with the same small brush, put dots, speckles or squiggles here and there over the rest of the can. If you have the know-how to draw stars, trees or some other Christmasy ideas, go to it. Use your imagination. Even little line drawings of smiling faces look tricky. I don't advise the use of "sparkle dust" or sequins or other elaborate additions; these tend to wash off or at least shed bits of sparkle whenever they are handled, and no one likes to eat a cookie full of gold dust.

A second method, faster but less personal than painting and decorating in one's own artistic style, calls for nothing more than a quick purchase of a couple of yards of self-adhesive vinyl cover, which comes usually eighteen inches wide with a backing that peels off the sticky side. This decorative material comes in many gold, green or red patterns suitable for Christmas.

Measure each can lengthwise between the two "rolled" edges of top and bottom; measure the circumference, allowing for an extra one-half inch for overlapping. Cut the vinyl to your measurements, peel off the backing as you wrap the vinyl around the can, and overlap the half-inch extra. If the can has a metal lid (instead of a plastic one which won't need covering) measure the metal lid, add an inch to the circle when you cut it, and make a few one-inch slits along the outer edge of the circle slanting toward the center. Lay the vinyl circle on a flat surface, peel off backing, center the lid on the sticky side and press down until it adheres. Then press up the edges to the rim. Cut off any excess along the rim. Neat, attractive and quick! No need to shudder at the thought of disclosing any lack of artistic ability with this method.

At the end of Chapter X, I've listed some tips to follow on packing and handling the contents of your cans, so store away the fancy containers until you get back from our cookie safari.

Chapter **VIII**

Before the Hoorah Starts Part 2

Helpful Hints

Now, while it's early in December and you are as fresh as those uncaught trophies will be, possessing a strong arm and the will to go hunting, begin with the Springerle.

To trap the really authentic Springerle, you should have an old German wooden block such as my Grandma handed down to me, carved in a traditional set of designs for imprinting the dough. Alas, these wooden blocks are scarcer than cheap Rembrandts although I've heard they may still be bought in the Pennsylvania Dutch area. But a good substitute can be bought in the form of a special Springerle rolling pin, with carved imprints for marking the dough, at any housewares section of a department store. If you can't find the special rolling pin, however, you can settle for the simple rolled cookies criss-crossed with a fork after cutting into squares.

No matter which kind you choose to trap, you must let the cookies "set" for several hours or overnight before baking. This is no drawback for it divides the stint of mixing, rolling and cutting from that of baking, cooling and storing.

Don't let the ingredient "powdered hartshorn" throw you. This is ammonium carbonate in powdered form, sometimes called "bakers' ammonia" and it can be purchased at any drug store. It is inexpensive, but buy only an ounce or so because it evaporates and hardens if exposed to air; be sure to keep it in a container with a screw-top, one that is air-tight, until used.

These anise-flavored perfections are especially superb when served with tea, coffee or Christmas wine. In fact, one can't resist dunking them for then they simply melt on the tongue like sugar-plums.

I've chosen Springerle as our first trophy because they are wonderful "keepers" and retain their flavor and freshness even when frozen a month ahead.

53. SPRINGERLE ("SELF-FROSTING")

1 lb. confectioner's (XXXX) sugar (2 cups)	1½ teaspoons powdered harts-horn (bakers' ammonia)
1 lb. sifted flour (4 cups)	2 tablespoons anise seed (crushed)
4 large eggs (room temperature)	Rind of 1 large lemon, grated

Beat eggs, sugar and grated lemon rind together for ½ hour by hand beating or 10 minutes by electric mixer until pale lemon-colored. Crush anise seed in small square of doubled cheesecloth with hammer or heavy object, and mix crushed seeds with sifted flour and powdered hartshorn. Add to egg and sugar mixture, beating in gradually and finishing by hand mixing. Dough should be stiff enough to handle without tearing when rolled.

Roll out on floured board to ⅛ inch thickness, using regular rolling pin. Then, using either carved wooden block or special

Springerle rolling pin, press or roll in the designs. Cut in squares marked by block or Springerle pin and lay out each square on paper towels or clean tea towels. NOTE: If using a plain rolling pin only, mark the flattened dough into squares, cut apart, and crisscross the top of each square with tines of a fork.

Let squares dry overnight or for several hours at room temperature. Then bake on floured (not oiled) cookie sheets in a moderately hot (375 degree) oven about 8 minutes or until bottoms are pale golden brown. Cool on wire rack or paper towels. Store in tightly lidded can. Makes about 10 dozen squares.

These cookies have a solid base with the design rising to a thin sugary crust on top. NOTE: If you prefer a sweeter cookie, roll out the dough in a mixture of 1 part flour and 1 part XXXX sugar.

• After spending the time needed to net your catch of Springerle (and I'm sure you'll agree it was time well spent after tasting them), I'll allow you an afternoon or evening of less intricate hunting by guiding you to the following two trophies. Both can be brought down with a minimum of effort and both may lie unbaked in the freezer awaiting the final slicing and baking at some future time, near the end of our safari. Or, if you prefer making them immediately, they keep very well in either freezer or cupboard as long as they are stored well-sealed from air and moisture in plastic wrap or freezer bag within a tightly lidded can.

The first, Rainbow Fruit Rounds, are the prettiest Christmasy little rounds ever and taste delicately delicious.

The second are rich golden brown trophies that rival the Springerle as a tea or coffee accompaniment, and their flavor is a heavenly blend of lemon and molasses that children as well as adults love.

54. RAINBOW FRUIT ROUNDS

1 cup margarine or butter
1 cup confectioner's sugar
  (XXXX)
1 large egg
2½ cups sifted flour
¼ teaspoon cream of tartar

¾ cup chopped nuts
¾ cup chopped candied fruit
½ cup whole red candied
  cherries
½ cup whole green candied
  cherries

Cream butter or margarine and sugar together. Add egg, blending thoroughly. Stir in flour and cream of tartar, again blending thoroughly. Pat out dough on a floured board to an oblong shape, about ½ inch thick. Scatter chopped nuts and candied fruit evenly over the dough and line up the whole cherries in alternate long rows of red and green from one end of the oblong to the other. This careful placing of the cherries will make the cookies' patterns of color more uniform. Roll up the dough beginning at one long side. Press together well to eliminate air pockets. Divide into two halves to make shorter, more easily handled, rolls. Wrap in plastic wrap and freeze.

When ready to bake, heat oven to 375 degrees. Slice rolls into rounds as thinly as possible with a sharp knife. Place on lightly greased cookie sheets. Bake 6 to 8 minutes. The cookies when baked should be a pale creamy shade; do not overbake to brown. Cool on wire rack or paper towels and store in a tightly lidded can. Makes about 10 dozen. NOTE: When packing these confections into your large storage can to await the assembling of all varieties into smaller gift cans, place sheets of wax paper between each layer of cookies to prevent an occasional piece of fruit from sticking to the fruit in the neighboring cookie, top or bottom. Attempting to separate two cookies stuck together causes breakage because they are very delicate.

55. LEM-MOL-OAT COOKIES

½ cup soft shortening	2 tablespoons black molasses
½ cup brown sugar	1 teaspoon vanilla
½ cup white sugar	1 cup sifted flour
1 medium egg	½ teaspoon soda
Rind of 1 large lemon, grated	½ teaspoon salt
	1¾ cups rolled oats

Mix together the shortening, sugar, egg, lemon rind, molasses and vanilla. Sift together the flour, soda and salt, and add to first mixture. Stir in the oats. This makes a stiff mixture which you may have to finish by mixing with your hands. Mold the dough into two rolls about 1½ inches in diameter. Wrap in plastic wrap and freeze until ready to be baked.

To bake, heat oven to 400 degrees. Slice frozen dough as thinly as possible (about ⅛ inch thick) with a thin sharp knife. Don't worry if slices are not exactly round; they tend to form oblongs when sliced as the dough warms very quickly. But since too many round cookies make your gift can monotonous, this variation makes an interesting change.

Place each slice on ungreased baking sheet about 1 inch apart. Bake 8 to 10 minutes. Do not let cookies get too brown. Cool on wire rack or paper towels, and store in tightly lidded can. Makes about 6 dozen cookies.

• Now you are well launched on this safari. A day of rest, perhaps, and you'll be eager to proceed. It is still early in the season so let's get up early in the morning to bag that elusive bird known as the Molasses Sand Tart. There are many versions of this crispiest of trophies and most are of the common domestic variety. But I am your guide and won't let you down with such ordinary game. Trophy #56 is extraordinary!

91

Aside from their mouth-watering goodness, these crispy little tarts have a marvelous keeping quality. If sealed inside plastic wrap or a plastic freezer bag in a tightly covered can, they will keep six weeks without loss of freshness or flavor. Moreover, if a few dozen are prudently held out and stored in the freezer (sealed in a can with freezer tape around the edge of the lid) they may be enjoyed months later. Your family and guests in spring or summer will call you a smart hostess.

Unless you hide away your trapped trophies, you may never have any left to freeze. You must develop a strong will to resist the pleas of your family for "just one little plate of cookies today"; and a strong lock on cupboard or freezer door will help. If you keep a list of the number of dozens you've brought down to date and deduct immediately each cookie gobbled up ahead of time, you'll see how quickly your totals diminish if you are weak-willed. A little simple arithmetic: forty dozen cookies divided by ten names on your list allows four dozen to each name. If you trap ten varieties, and your family nibbles just one dozen of each kind during December, you are reduced to only three dozen per gift can. So *watch it,* and watch those foxy marauders, too.

56. MOLASSES SAND TARTS

2 cups flour
⅔ cup sugar
⅔ cup softened butter or
    margarine
½ cup unsulphured black
    molasses

1 egg yolk*
    topping mix:
½ cup sugar
1½ teaspoons cinnamon
    rolling out mix:
½ cup confectioners sugar
½ cup flour

Sift flour and sugar together. Melt butter over low heat and add molasses. Remove from heat, cool and add egg yolk. Blend. Add molasses mixture to flour and sugar mixture; mix till dough resembles pastry dough. Chill or freeze overnight, or if you really began early in the morning, chill or freeze for six hours.

When ready to bake, lay a two-foot long sheet of plastic wrap (Handi-Wrap resists splitting or tearing and is easier to handle than the kind that clings) on a dampened counter or table top. Sprinkle a little rolling mix (see above) on the plastic wrap. Using a small portion of the chilled or frozen dough, place in center of plastic wrap and cover with another sheet of wrap. Roll very thin (⅛ inch or less if possible). Press star or tree cookie cutter *on top of plastic wrap;* it will cut through the dough but not the wrap! When all cookies under the wrap are cut, carefully remove the top sheet. Lift out unnecessary bits and edges around cookies. Then move each cookie to baking sheet, using a pancake turner. If you can space each cookie while cutting out the shapes to have the finished batch fit your baking sheet, you can eliminate using the pancake turner. Simply peel off the top sheet of wrap, remove bits and edges from around cookie shapes, lay your greased baking sheet over the shapes, and holding each end of plastic wrap flip over entire batch on to the baking sheet. Press lightly on each shape so it will adhere to baking sheet, and then peel off the second sheet of plastic wrap.

*Use egg white in Trophy #70 (Beacon Hills) or in #71 (Swiss Nut Kisses).

Of course, if you don't have any plastic wrap, you simply roll out a small portion at a time on your pastry board, using the rolling mix, and also using the pancake turner to transfer the cookies to your cookie sheet to bake. This old-fashioned method is fine but causes much more cleaning-up and takes much longer.

Sprinkle the cookie shapes with topping mix (see above) and bake 6 minutes in a 400-degree oven. Cool on wire rack or paper towels and store in a tightly lidded can. Makes about 10 dozen tarts.

• Let's move right along to bring down three delicious *real butter* trophies, each acquired by a different method of hunting.

Lemon Pecan Thins are little rounds sliced from a chilled or frozen roll, flavored with a delicate lemon-nutty blend. Christmas Butter Fancies, rolled and cut into holiday shapes, and Vaniljek-ranse, shaped through a star-disk with a cookie press into rings, are rich buttery confections. The Fancies are not at all like the flour-y mixtures that pass for sugar cookies in so many cook books, but are the true old-fashioned favorites dating back to the days when butter was plentiful and cheap.

Real butter *must* be used for all three trophies, no substitutes, but the results are well worth the added cost.

Mo-
lasses
Sand
Tarts

57. LEMON PECAN THINS

$\frac{1}{2}$ cup butter (no substitutes)
1 cup sugar
1 medium egg, well-beaten
$1\frac{1}{2}$ tablespoons grated lemon
  rind

$1\frac{1}{2}$ tablespoons lemon juice
2 cups flour
$\frac{1}{4}$ teaspoon salt
1 teaspoon baking powder
1 cup pecans, chopped

Cream butter and sugar thoroughly. Stir in beaten egg, lemon juice and grated rind. Beat well. Sift flour, salt and baking powder together and add to the egg-sugar-butter mixture; blend well. Stir in nut meats.

Shape into two rolls about $1\frac{1}{2}$ inches in diameter, wrap in plastic wrap, and chill or freeze until rolls are solid to touch. Slice with a thin, sharp knife into $\frac{1}{8}$ inch or less rounds. Bake on greased cookie sheet in moderate (350 degree) oven for 12-14 minutes. Do not overbrown. Makes about 5 dozen cookies. Cool on a wire rack or paper towels, and store in a tightly lidded can.

58. CHRISTMAS BUTTER FANCIES

1 cup butter (no substitutes)
1 cup sugar
2 cups sifted flour

2 teaspoons flavoring
  (vanilla, almond, lemon
  or rum extract)

Blend butter and sugar together thoroughly. Add sifted flour, a little at a time, and desired flavoring a drop or two at a time. Chill dough in refrigerator for two hours. Then roll one-third the dough at a time to $\frac{1}{8}$ inch thickness on a board sprinkled with 1 part flour and 1 part confectioners sugar. Cut into Christ-mas shapes with cookie cutters. Carefully remove shapes with a pancake turner or wide spatula to ungreased baking sheets. Bake in 400 degree oven for 8 to 9 minutes. The little cookies should not be browned; remove when they are a pale tan around edges. Cool on a wire rack or paper towels, and store in a tightly lidded can. Makes from 3 dozen to 6 dozen, according to size of cutter used.

59. VANILJEKRANSE

4½ cups sifted flour
   1 cup sugar
   1 cup blanched, roasted
     almonds

1½ cups butter
   1 medium egg, beaten
   1 tablespoon vanilla

Drop shelled almonds into boiling water for three minutes. Cover with cold water, then slip off skins. Chop almonds finely (or grind in blender for 15 seconds) and spread on aluminum foil. Toast in hot oven till lightly browned.

Combine toasted chopped almonds, flour and sugar. Cut in butter until mixture has a corn meal consistency. Add beaten egg and vanilla; mix well. Turn out on a lightly floured board or onto a sheet of plastic wrap on a dampened counter or table top, and knead until smooth. Chill for one hour.

Using cookie press and star-shaped disk, press dough into long strips onto lightly floured surface, either board or plastic wrap. Cut into 4-inch pieces and shape each piece into a ring or wreath. Lift onto lightly-greased cookie sheets. Bake in a quick moderate (375 degree) oven for 12 to 15 minutes, until edges are golden. Cool on a wire rack or paper towels, and store in a tightly lidded can. Makes about 8 dozen.

● Ready to go out for the trophy that ends the first week on safari? At least thirty-five years ago my sister, a young beginner, guided me to these scrumptious treats, Elfin Faces. After adding a change or two of my own devising, I captured an award from a newspaper cookie contest for this trophy and have the yellowed clipping still in my scrapbook. Beginners, now that you know mere children (Sister and I) were successful, have no hesitation about trying these little critters. They are fruity but crisp snaps that are excellent keepers, never losing their fresh flavor even if brought down a month ahead of time. And catching them is a snap, too, if you'll forgive the pun.

60. ELFIN FACES

1½ cups sugar (half may be
    brown sugar if desired)
1 cup butter or margarine
3 eggs
1 cup raisins (seedless)
½ cup black molasses
3 cups flour*
1 teaspoon soda
1 teaspoon salt

1 teaspoon ground cloves
1 teaspoon ground cinnamon
1 teaspoon ground allspice
For decorating with faces:
    Nutmeats in fairly large
      pieces
    Extra raisins
    Green and red candied
      cherries, sliced

Cream butter and sugar together. Stir in the 3 unbeaten eggs, one at a time. Then add molasses. Sift together flour, salt, soda and spices, and add gradually to mixture. Stir in raisins. Drop by scant teaspoonfuls on lightly oiled cookie sheet. Make faces on each cookie by using slices of cherries for mouths, nutmeats for noses and raisins for eyes. Press decorations into dough fairly deep to prevent possible scorching. Bake in 375 degree oven for 8-10 minutes.

Cool on wire rack or paper towels, and store in a tightly lidded can lined with plastic wrap. Separate each layer of cookies with wax paper to prevent the cherry slices on each cookie from sticking to others. Makes 12 to 14 dozen.

*You may have to add another ¼ cup flour to the dough if you used large eggs. Check the first sheet of cookies; if they spread out to lose shape because of the extra moisture in the large eggs, add the extra flour to the rest of the dough. When baked, these cookies should be firm but not browned.

Chapter **IX**

Laces and Fancies

More Cookies

Now I'd like to guide you to six trophies which are in the category of birds of paradise. These are the rare and beautiful prizes which give a unique class to your gift selection. Unusual and colorful though they be, not one is too difficult to trap even for the beginner.

Trophy #61 is indeed a miracle mixture for from one bowl of basic dough come four batches of cookies, each batch different from the others in texture, appearance and flavor but all equally delicious.

The real Christmas touch to your gift assortment is Trophy #62, Maggi's Striped Candy Canes. These little wonders can be (and usually are) eaten by the handful like peanuts, but this trophy furnishes quite a few canes for a dozen gift cans if you

98

don't make the canes larger than instructed. A few of these canes in small plastic boxes such as those used for bobby pins are a delightful surprise in a child's Christmas stocking, and are much better for them than candy if gobbled up before breakfast on Christmas morning.

The "Laces" of this chapter's title are astonishing to the hunter in the way they are brought down and in their appearance and taste. If you don't make both kinds you'll be sorry, for both disappear like snow in spring. In fact, I've seldom had any of either left for freezing until spring!

61. JAN'S FOUR-IN-ONE MIRACLE COOKIES

Basic Miracle Dough:

2½ cups flour	¾ cup vegetable oil
1½ teaspoons baking powder	(polyunsaturated)
¾ teaspoon salt	1 cup sugar
	2 medium eggs

Combine oil and sugar in a large bowl. Add unbeaten eggs and mix thoroughly. Sift flour, baking powder and salt together and add all at once to mixture in large bowl. Mix thoroughly by hand as dough will be stiff. Divide dough into four parts.

PART I RED NUTMEG DAINTIES

Additions:

1 teaspoon vanilla   ½ teaspoon ground nutmeg
   red sugar crystals or garnishettes

To one-fourth above dough, add vanilla and nutmeg. Mix well. Oil palms of hands to handle dough. Shape into small balls (approximately one teaspoon heaped or one scant tablespoon for each ball) and dip tops of balls in red sugar crystals or garnishettes. Flatten balls slightly with fork after placing on lightly oiled cookie sheets. Bake 10 minutes in 375 degree oven. Do not brown. Cool on wire rack or paper towels.

99

Additions:

1 tablespoon almond
    flavoring
  Green vegetable food
    coloring

⅓ cup confectioner's
    sugar

To one-fourth above dough, add almond flavoring mixed with the green food coloring. Blend in, then add the sugar. Mix well. Using tree-shape plate in cookie press, press out the little trees onto ungreased cookie sheet. Bake 10 minutes in 375 degree oven. Do not brown. Cool on wire rack or paper towels.

PART III GOLDEN LEMON STARS

Additions:

1 tablespoon lemon juice (or 1 teaspoon lemon extract)
  Grated rind of one lemon   ⅓ cup confectioner's sugar
  Yellow vegetable food
    coloring

To one-fourth basic dough, add the lemon juice or extract, grated lemon rind and several drops of yellow food coloring. Mix well, then blend in sugar. Roll out on board dusted with confectioner's sugar (or between two sheets of plastic wrap dusted with confectioner's sugar) to ⅛ inch thickness and cut out cookies with star-shaped cutter. Transfer to lightly oiled cookie sheet with pancake turner or wide spatula. Bake 7-8 minutes in 375 degree oven. Do not let these delicate golden stars brown. Cool on wire rack or paper towels.

PART IV CHOCOLATE-PEANUT FINGERS

Additions:

⅓ cup peanut butter	1 package semi-sweet
⅓ cup brown sugar	chocolate bits
½ teaspoon baking soda	1 cup peanuts

To remaining basic dough, stir in the peanut butter. Mix baking soda with brown sugar and add to dough. Blend well. Oil palms of hands to handle dough. Roll small balls (1 rounded teaspoonful or 1 scant tablespoonful each) between palms until lengthened into cylinders. Place on ungreased cookie sheets about an inch apart, and flatten slightly with fork lengthwise. Bake 10 minutes in 375 degree oven. Cool on brown paper or paper towels.

While cooling cookies, melt 1 package semi-sweet chocolate bits over hot water (do not let chocolate get too hot) and chop 1 cup peanuts medium fine. Dip one end of cool cookie first into melted chocolate, then into chopped peanuts. Do not coat cookies more than half their length. Harden on waxed paper.

VARIATIONS ON PART IV:

Dip in melted butterscotch bits or caramel bits, or the new peanut butter bits. Roll in chopped walnuts or chopped almonds.

This miracle-trophy makes about 12 dozen cookies, or approximately three dozen of each kind. The amount may vary by as much as a few dozen, depending on the size of the mold-plate, cutter, cylinder or ball measured for each kind. No matter, you will wish you had doubled the quantity when you see the results and taste each variation.

Store each variety separately in tightly lidded large cans until you are ready to re-pack in gift cans.

62. MAGGI'S STRIPED CANDY CANES

1 cup butter or margarine
1 cup sifted confectioner's
    sugar
1 large egg
2 teaspoons almond flavoring

1 teaspoon vanilla
2½ cups sifted flour
1 teaspoon salt
red and yellow food coloring

Combine shortening, confectioner's sugar, egg and flavorings. Mix thoroughly. Stir in sifted flour and salt, blending well. Divide dough in two parts equally.

Blend several drops of red coloring in one portion of dough, and yellow coloring in the other half. Make one red and one yellow roll, each the length of your cookie press, and insert the two rolls carefully, one *beside* the other, into cookie press. Use small star disk. Press out, shaping into cane shape, on ungreased cookie sheets. Make canes small, one inch for the curved tops and two inches for the straight parts. The two colors should come out fairly evenly, side by side. Bake about 9 minutes or until edges turn very lightly golden, in 375 degree oven. Remove with pancake turner while still warm, and place on wire rack or paper towels to cool. Store in layers in tightly lidded can lined with plastic wrap. Be sure the wrap is long enough to be folded over at the top, to keep out any moistness. These are crispy little critters and should remain that way.

See the next page for a tasty variation of this recipe, one that evidently (from its name) was discovered and hunted by the Russians, possibly in the time of Catherine the Great.

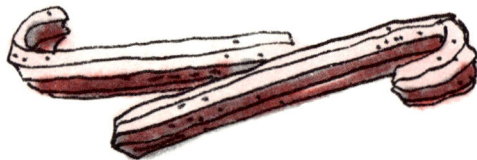

63. RUSSIAN NUTTY CANES

2¼ cups flour
⅔ cup pecans or peanuts
1 cup butter or margarine

½ cup confectioner's sugar
¼ teaspoon salt
1 teaspoon vanilla

Sift flour; measure. Chop nuts fine. Cream butter or margarine. Gradually add nuts and sugar to softened shortening and blend till fluffy. Add flour, salt and vanilla, mixing well. Start oven at 400 degrees or hot.

Break off small pieces of dough and roll into cylinders between hands. Shape into little canes, one inch of curved top and two inches of straight shaft. Bake on ungreased cookie sheets for about 10 minutes. Do not overbrown. While warm, roll in confectioner's sugar.

A change from the cane shape is the icicle. Instead of shaping into canes, twist the cylinder in a spiral shape, pointing one end slightly. Sprinkle with granulated sugar before baking. Cool on paper towels and store in a tightly lidded can lined with plastic wrap. Fold top of wrap over twice to protect from any air or moisture.

64. DUTCH CARAWAY COOKIES

2 cups sifted flour
2 teaspoons baking powder
¼ teaspoon salt
   Grated rind of 1 large
   lemon

½ cup butter or margarine
1 cup sugar
1 large egg
2 teaspoons caraway seeds

Cream shortening until fluffy. Gradually add sugar while beating mixture. Beat in egg. Sift flour and remeasure to exactly two cups. Add baking powder and salt to remeasured flour. Sift again. Sprinkle grated rind of lemon on top of flour mixture. Put caraway seeds into a small doubled square of cheesecloth, fold over cloth and pound seeds with hammer or other heavy object to crush and release flavor. Sprinkle pounded seeds onto flour mixture.

Mix flour, rind and seeds thoroughly into bowl of wet ingredients. Chill for at least one hour. Put chilled dough through cookie press, using any disk desired. Bake in 350 degree oven for 11-12 minutes. Do not brown. Cool on wire rack or paper towels and store in tightly lidded can lined with plastic wrap (or in plastic bag fitted inside can. Twist top of bag closed or use rubber band to close bag before putting on lid of can.)

Suggestion: A few drops of red food coloring to turn dough pink may be added before chilling. Press through flower disk, accent petal curves with slivers of blanched almonds, and press a few whole caraway seeds into center of flower, or a bit of glazed red cherry. Of course, any coloring may be chosen, but let me caution you about one color with the following little verse:

Y-y-ick-k!

(apologies to Gelett Burgess and his purple cow)

I've never seen a cookie *blue;*
If seen, I'll never take one.
And on that subject I'm not through:
I swear I'll never bake one.

If you should see a cookie blue
Be sure you don't select it.
Your teeth and tongue may turn this hue;
Your tummy may reject it.

65. BLACK WALNUT LACE ROLL 'EM UPS

½ cup maple flavored corn
    syrup
(½ teaspoon maple flavoring
    added to white corn
    syrup)
½ cup brown sugar,
    packed in cup

10 tablespoons butter
¾ cup sifted flour
¾ cup finely chopped
    black walnuts

Combine butter, sugar and syrup in saucepan over low heat, and stir till butter and sugar melt. Remove from heat and blend in flour and nuts. Batter will be on the thin side. Drop by scant teaspoonfuls onto ungreased cookie sheets, allowing several inches between cookies to keep them separated. They spread considerably.

I would advise baking no more than five or six at a time because they must be handled while fairly hot, to roll them up. Bake 7-8 minutes in 350 degree oven.

Allow cookies to cool *no more* than 30 seconds after removing from oven. If you have tender fingers that hate to handle a hot cookie, keep a saucer of chilled salad oil handy along with a paper towel. When you are ready to pick up the hot cookie, dip finger-tips in the cold oil, blot excess oil on the paper towel, and grab away. Working quickly, remove cookie with pancake turner, grasp at one side, then roll into a clothespin-sized roll. If the last few cookies on the sheet cool too much and become too crisp to roll, pop them back in the oven a moment to soften again. Place each cookie as soon as rolled on paper towel with rolled edge down. Store when completely cool in a tightly lidded can lined with

Black Walnut

plastic wrap. Fold wrap over at top of can to seal out humidity; these cookies become soft and sticky instead of remaining crisp and crunchy if air gets to them while stored.

Remember, when these cookies are baking they spread out very flat like a pancake, get bubbly on top (this makes the "Lace") and look somewhat like candy. After a moment's cooling out of the oven they begin to crisp up rapidly. Remember to work quickly with them. This trophy nets about 5 dozen roll 'em ups, two inches long.

66. ALMOND LACE ROLL 'EM UPS

1 cup unblanched almonds	*¾ cup sugar*
¾ cup butter or margarine	*1½ tablespoons milk*
1½ tablespoons cream	*6 tablespoons flour*

Finely chop, grind or place in blender for 15 seconds the unblanched almonds. Mix ground nuts, sugar and flour together in saucepan. Cut in butter or margarine coarsely, then add cream and milk. Stir over low fire in heavy pan or skillet till butter melts. Remove from fire and drop by scant teaspoonfuls at least three inches apart on a well-oiled cookie sheet. Make no more than five or six at a time. Bake at 350 degrees about 9 minutes. Cookies should be slightly brown at edges and bubbling in centers. Let cool half a minute or so until edge is beginning to "set." Lift each cookie off sheet with pancake turner, roll from one edge to the other in a clothespin-shaped roll, and place, edge down, on brown paper or paper towels to cool.

If your tender fingers rebel at handling the hot cookies, dip fingers in a saucer of chilled salad oil, blot on paper towel, and then roll cookie. *Work quickly.* If the last cookie on the baking sheet gets too cool and crisp before you roll it up, pop the sheet back into the oven for a minute till the cookie becomes pliable again. This makes about 4½ dozen two-inch long cookies. If you make them smaller, cut baking time to 7-8 minutes. Store in tightly covered can lined with plastic wrap. Fold wrap at top.

107

Chapter X

The Last Mile

It's Nearly Christmas!

Here we go into the final frenetic rush before the big day. Our safari is almost over but the last side trip or two ought to fill any remaining empty cans. And the varieties begging to be bagged are not only some of the most tempting eye-fillers ever but they are expeditious-sialagogic-supersplendidoshious, or in other words, quick, tasty magic.

The carols resound from TV and radio; cedar and pine and spruce spread their heady aromas around every street corner; festive cards are arriving with greetings from relatives and friends from every corner of the globe and perhaps from the moon by the time you read this. All over town poor souls are scurrying hither and yon in a desperate search for *something* — for the boss, the visiting fireman, the forgotten cousin or maybe even you.

Take an evening to count your blessings while pitying those poor souls. You have a bulging gift closet of stacked trophies in glass, jar and can. After counting, be on the safe side; read over these last-minute trophies so you can hie forth tomorrow to lay in any ammunition you need to capture the magic quickies that round out your collection.

Trophy #67 is a crisp drop cookie which adds orange flavor and color to your variety. Another marvelous orange-flavored drop cookie is #68, a rich nutty concoction. An interesting and delicious trophy, #69, is made in a jelly-roll pan or other shallow baking pan. Instead of using the time-consuming method of rolling out the dough and cutting special shapes, you simply cut the entire batch of baked dough into odd sizes to suit your fancy. A true last-minute quickie to fill out your gift needs!

Beacon Hills and Swiss Nut Kisses are wondrous meringue-type mounds that call for egg whites but not yolks. You may use the yolks in Trophy #56 (Molasses Sand Tarts) or in custards, sauces, omelets, etc. later on if you strain them, add a dash of salt, and freeze them in small plastic containers until needed. If you plan to use the yolks in the next day or so, keep them covered with a small amount of water in a jar in the refrigerator.

Sandy Poofs must derive their name from the fact that they literally explode into delicious tiny melting bits when eaten. Or perhaps they are called "poofs" because they disappear so quickly when served with wine or tea. Don't expect to have any left for freezing after Christmas!

I learned to hunt Trophy #72 with Beth, a hunter who has been bagging them for more than thirty years. These luscious little drops are well worth the trip if you will follow me to their capture. And I learned how to run down the last of the drop trophies, #74, so long ago that I've forgotten who was my guide. The origin of these old-time currant goodies is the Pennsylvania Dutch country; perhaps they are still being bagged there where goodness is never "all."

67. ORANGE FLAKE COOKIES

⅓ cup butter or margarine
½ cup sugar
  1 large egg, well-beaten
  1 cup sifted flour
  1 teaspoon baking powder
½ teaspoon salt

3 tablespoons orange juice
Grated rind of two oranges
1 cup wheat flake cereal
½ cup corn flake crumbs
6 drops yellow food coloring
  (optional: garnishettes)

Cream butter or margarine, add sugar gradually, then add beaten egg. Sift together flour, baking powder and salt, and add alternately with orange juice to creamed mixture. Add yellow food coloring and blend well. Stir in grated orange rind and cereal flakes and crumbs. Mix well. Drop by scant teaspoonfuls onto well-greased cookie sheets. These little flaked cookies may be made even more decorative if you sprinkle a few multicolored garnishettes on top before baking. Garnishettes may be found in small jars or packages in grocery stores. Bake in 375 degree oven about 12 minutes or until edges become lightly browned. Cool on wire rack or paper towels. Makes about 4 dozen.

For storage after thoroughly cooling the cookies, line a large can with plastic wrap (or stack the cookies in the can in a half-gallon size plastic freezer bag; fasten top of bag with rubber band). Be sure your can has a tight lid, also, for these little flakes are best when they are crisp, and moisture in the air will soften them in a day if they are not stored properly.

68. NUTTY ORANGE ROUNDS

1/2 cup butter or margarine	1 cup rolled oats
1 cup brown sugar, packed	1 cup sifted flour
1 large egg	1/2 teaspoon soda
2 tablespoons orange juice	1/2 teaspoon salt
1 tablespoon grated orange rind	1/2 cup chopped nuts (optional) 1/2 cup raisins

Cream butter or margarine and sugar together. Add egg and blend well. Add orange juice and grated rind alternately with rolled oats. Measure a cup of sifted flour, then resift with soda and salt into mixture. Add nuts (and raisins if wanted) and mix again thoroughly.

Drop by scant teaspoonfuls onto greased or oiled baking sheets. Bake 12 minutes at 350 degrees. Makes about 4 dozen. Cool on wire rack or paper towels. Store in plastic-wrap lined can with tight lid.

These little critters may be decorated with extra nuts and raisins similar to Elfin Faces (Trophy #60) or with candied orange peel faces. Cut orange peel into thin slivers to make the faces, and press into dough before baking the cookies. If using candied orange peel, store each layer of cookies between waxed paper to prevent cookies from sticking together while stored.

69. PEANUT BRITTLE COOKIES

1 package (5 1/2 oz.) peanut butter chips	1 large egg, slightly beaten
	1 teaspoon vanilla
1/2 cup butter or margarine	1 cup unsifted flour
1/2 cup brown sugar, packed in cup	1/2 teaspoon baking powder
	1/2 teaspoon cinnamon

Over hot water, melt 1/2 cup of the peanut butter chips until they lose their shape when stirred. Blend butter or margarine, brown sugar, 2 tablespoons of the beaten egg and vanilla until fluffy. Add melted peanut butter chips. Stir in unsifted flour, baking powder and cinnamon; mix well.

Spread dough into an ungreased jelly-roll pan (15 by 10 inch size) or make a rectangle about 14 by 10 inches on an ungreased baking sheet. Brush top with remaining egg and sprinkle with remaining peanut butter chips. Bake in a 325 degree oven for about 20 minutes or until lightly browned. Cool slightly, then cut into uneven shapes.

Makes about 4 dozen small shapes. When thoroughly cooled, store in a can lined with plastic wrap. Fold plastic wrap closely over cookies and be sure the can has a tight lid.

70. BEACON HILL COOKIES

1 cup semi-sweet chocolate
    chips
2 large egg whites
⅛ teaspoon salt
½ cup sugar

½ teaspoon vanilla
½ teaspoon vinegar
1 cup chopped walnuts
Halved walnut meats

Melt chocolate chips in double boiler. While melting chips, beat egg whites with salt till foamy. Gradually add sugar while beating. When stiff peaks form, add vanilla and vinegar, and then fold in the melted chocolate chips and the chopped walnuts.

Drop by scant teaspoonfuls on well-oiled cookie sheet; decorate each mound with ½ walnut meat. Bake in 350 degree oven for about 10 minutes. Cool on wire rack or paper towels and store in a plastic freezer bag fitted inside a tightly lidded can. Makes about 3½ dozen.

71. SWISS NUT KISSES

1 cup finely ground hazel nuts (filberts) & 3 dozen whole filberts
⅓ cup flour
4 egg whites
½ cup sugar

2 squares semi-sweet
    (melted) chocolate

Sift flour before measuring; mix ⅓ cup flour with finely ground nuts. Beat egg whites until stiff enough to hold a soft peak. Gradually add sugar, beating until mixture forms stiff peaks. Gently fold in the mixture of flour and ground nuts.

Drop by teaspoonfuls onto baking sheets lined with well-oiled paper or oiled aluminum foil.

Bake in a 375 degree oven about 15 minutes or until lightly brown. Cool on wire rack or waxed paper. While kisses are cooling, melt the chocolate over hot water. Decorate each mound with a filbert dipped in the melted chocolate. When chocolate nuts harden, store cookies in tightly lidded can lined with plastic wrap. Makes about 3 dozen.

113

72. BETH'S CHOCOLATE-OAT DROPS

3/4 cup butter or margarine
1/2 cup brown sugar, packed in cup
1/2 cup granulated sugar
2 large eggs
1 cup and 2 tablespoons flour
1 teaspoon baking powder
1/4 teaspoon salt

1/3 cup milk
1 teaspoon vanilla
1/2 cup walnuts, chopped
1 bar semi-sweet chocolate
  (or 1 package chocolate
  bits)
3 cups uncooked oats

Cream butter or margarine and both sugars. Beat in eggs, one at a time. Sift flour, baking powder and salt together and add to creamed mixture alternately with milk. Stir in vanilla and add nuts, oats and chocolate. Drop on oiled cookie sheets by heaping teaspoonfuls, and bake in 375 degree oven for about 12 minutes.

These delicacies may be decorated with a half walnut, or sprinkled with a few chocolate "jimmies" or garnishettes. Makes about 7 dozen. Cool cookies on wire rack or paper towels, and store in a tightly lidded can lined with plastic wrap. Fold plastic wrap over tops of cookies to help keep out moisture.

73. SANDY POOFS

1 cup butter
1/2 cup confectioner's sugar
2 teaspoons vanilla
2 1/4 cups sifted flour

1 cup finely chopped pecans
  or butternuts
  (Brazil nuts)
1 tablespoon water

Cream butter and sugar together. When fluffy, add vanilla and water. Gradually add flour. When dough becomes too stiff

to mix by beaters, finish by hand mixing. Add finely chopped nuts; mix thoroughly.

Oil palms of hands slightly. Roll 1 scant tablespoon each into small balls. These little balls do not spread so they may be placed fairly closely together on ungreased cookie sheets. Bake in 350 degree oven for about 15-18 minutes or until they show pale brown on the bottoms. Turn one or two over after baking 15 minutes to check, and remove from oven immediately if pale brown. Do not overbake.

Cool on paper towels or brown paper. When thoroughly cool, roll in confectioner's sugar before storing in tightly lidded can. Line can with plastic wrap, and fold over top of cookies. Makes about 5 dozen.

74. OLD-TIME CHRISTMAS CURRANT DROPS

1 cup sugar	1/8 teaspoon salt
1 cup butter	1 cup currants
3 large eggs	1 large lemon rind, grated
1¾ cups flour	Juice of ½ lemon

Cream butter and sugar together, then add eggs, one at a time. Add a little flour (about ½ cup) with lemon rind and juice. Mix ½ cup flour with salt and currants. Add with rest of flour, alternately, until all of flour and currants are used. Grease or oil cookie sheets heavily.

Slide cookie sheets into 350 degree oven for a minute or two before dropping teaspoonfuls of the cookie dough onto them. Heating the cookie sheets makes the dough melt a bit and makes the proper "thin edge" which distinguishes these cookies. Bake in 350 degree oven for about 12 minutes. When cookies are golden-brown around edges and pale cream-colored in centers, they are baked. Remove from sheets with pancake turner while cookies are still very warm, and cool on brown paper or paper towels. Store in tightly lidded can lined with plastic wrap. Makes about 7 dozen.

Chapter **XI**

Christmas Melange
Packaging Your Cookies

I'm ready to call it a day (or a month) and bring you back from our safari with your game-bag full of crispy trophies worthy of the most critical expert.

But I can't leave you without a few words of warning on two other pitfalls which may lie in your path, sooner or later. I know there are birds in the bush I've ignored, fine ones perhaps and tasty, too. But they *may* have peculiarities, tendencies to dry out or get soggy, to lose flavor, to disappoint in a dozen unexpected ways after being stored for a time.

If Aunt Gatrooda or some other well-meaning hunter insists on guiding you to her favorite Christmas cookie trophy to add to your collection, go along with thanks, of course, but with reservations. Bag a batch of the new wonders long before you begin your next Christmas safari. Try them out on your long-suffering family first. Sock a few away in one of those good old tightly lidded cans. Wait a couple of weeks and then get them out to check. If they have dried out, lost flavor or even, horrible thought, gotten moldy (some bar cookies, the moist fruity kind, particularly, may mold in a short time unless kept frozen) *don't* force them to live cheek-by-jowl with your tested trophies in a gift can! One wrong type of cookie can lend its troubles to your crisp beauties, ruining weeks of effort and bringing down on your unsuspecting head a really low reputation as a cook and hunter.

Assuming you've taken the above warning to heart, you may still not be safe. An urge to show off your decorating prowess with *iced* cookies may lead you astray. There are very few icings for cookies which will weather the test of time, and those which contain water, milk or other liquids may sog up your crispies no end. Particularly, I caution you against careless icing of Sugar Cookies; hunters are more tempted to gild their lily-white surfaces than any other, and these cookies are the most vulnerable of all to the moisture in icings.

However, if you *must* try your hand at decorating, here is one icing trophy which seems to work rather well. Note that it contains no liquid per se except a smidgen of vanilla.

75. ORNAMENTAL FROSTING FOR COOKIES

2½ *cups confectioner's sugar* ¼ *teaspoon vanilla*
 ¼ *teaspoon cream of tartar* *(optional) food coloring*
 2 *medium egg whites*

Sift together sugar and cream of tartar. Beat egg whites until very stiff and gradually add the sugar-cream of tartar mixture. When very stiff, drizzle in the wee bit of vanilla and a drop of food coloring if desired. Put in cake-icing press, using any desired disc, and decorate cookies sparingly.

If you make this icing ahead of time, you must cover the bowl immediately with plastic wrap or a damp cloth until ready to use as it dries out quickly.

Do not decorate on a rainy day or when humidity is rampant. Pick a nice sunny day or a night when the stars are twinkly-clear. Spread out iced cookies singly until icing hardens, but do not let cookies stay out overnight on the table or wherever you place them

117

to dry as they will pick up moisture from the air even in dry weather. An hour or two should suffice to harden the icing. Then store in layers, with plastic wrap or waxed paper between, in a tightly lidded can lined with plastic wrap. Crispness in cookies is ephemeral — treat it with respect and care.

• Now you have finished your hunting, packed away all your gear and are ready to sort your trophies into individual gift cans.

The first, most important step is to see that the interiors of your gift cans are clean and dry. Cookie cans are *very* difficult to dry thoroughly. If you washed them before putting them away until needed but did not let them dry inside thoroughly, they will greet you with rust rims at the seams. Moisture lurks in those tiny seams beyond reach of towels. The simplest sure system is the oven-dry one. Light the oven to about 300 degrees before washing the cans. After drying them with a clean tea towel, place the cans and lids in the oven for a few minutes to let the heat penetrate the seams to dry up every bit of moisture. Remove, let cool thoroughly before putting on lids, and store in a dry place.

If you wash the cans just before packing cookies in them, this preliminary procedure is doubly necessary, even when lining the cans with plastic wrap. *Don't take chances with moisture.*

It is time now to discuss the best way to pack your gift cans. Christmas cookies made from recipes in this book can be safely packed days ahead to eliminate that last-minute rush, if you follow these instructions.

First of all, if you have made any side trips on your own to bring down soft, chewy cookies or those containing moist fruits, you *must* wrap these *individually* in plastic wrap before packing them with the crisp ones.

Secondly, cookies from the freezer should be allowed to come to room temperature before packing.

Thirdly, pack them if possible when the weather is clear and dry.

Put a ½ inch layer of Easter grass or crumpled tissue wrap in the bottom of each gift can. Then fit plastic freezer bags inside each can, or line each can with plastic wrap leaving enough at the top to fold over cookies.

Pack cookies carefully. The thicker flat cookies and drop kinds are best on the bottom as they resist breakage best. Thinner flat ones should be packed on the next layers, although you may fill in any open spaces with small drop cookies. Delicate kinds, such as Sandy Poofs, Rainbow Fruit Rounds and the Lace Roll 'em Ups should be packed near the top, fitting the Poofs into odd corners and gaps. Reserve the striped canes and green almond trees for the very top layer as they add Christmas color and theme to the assortment. An extra touch of color can be added also by packing a few tiny foil-wrapped chocolate bells, balls or Santas which can be bought at the candy counter in department stores, or red and green hard candies in the very small spaces left around the edges. When properly packed, no cookie or candy will move when the can is tipped or shaken.

Fold over the top of the plastic wrap to seal out air, or snap small rubber bands around the tops of the freezer bags if used. Put lids on cans. An extra precaution can be taken by putting either cellophane tape or freezer tape around the edge of each lid where it meets the can, after closing.

Cover the tape around the edge with inch-wide ribbon, tying it in a bow-knot on one side, and attach the gift tag. Remember, if you pack a special variety for Aunt Gatrooda or Cousin Zeke, mark it immediately after packing. Otherwise your toothless relative may receive a can of the nuttiest trophies instead of the nutless ones.

Finally, when packed, your gift cans should be stored in a safe place where they won't be knocked over, dropped, kicked against, moved about or subjected to extremes in temperature.

The hoorah and the shouting have ended. Your shelves are piled high with gaily wrapped delectable holiday gifts, neatly tagged except for a few extra unmarked ones reserved for emergencies — the unexpected guest, the forgotten friend, or perhaps a plea from some charitable organization for a "benefit" gift.

119

Now give yourself the gift you've envied Other People for
having. I mean that uncluttered quiet period of time just before
the Big Day when you are able to sit down without a worry about
your gift list, when you really arrive at a holiday frame of mind.

Watch old Scrooge and Amahl, if you like, on TV. Look at
your piled-up Christmas cards, really look at each one and think
of the sender. Listen to carols, really listen! Be reckless — have
your favorite drink and a handful of your best cookies before the
holiday horde makes its inroads.

To help evoke a holiday mood, I've added a seasonable poem
for you to mull over while waiting for Christmas.

BRINGING IN YE OLDE LOG

'Twas the eve before Christmas, and safe in their beds
Were all the grandchildren with unsnowed-on heads.

Grandma in her kerchief, Grandpop with no key
Went out in the backyard to bring in the tree,

When what to their frostbitten ears did resound
But the slam of the door ere they both turned around.

With mouths hanging open they stared at the house.
No one could get in, not even a mouse.

So up to the roof Grandpop went by a ladder
While Gran stood in snow with her false teeth a-chatter.

He climbed in a window, tripped over a chair,
And the children woke up thinking Santa was there.

He fled down the steps to throw open the door;
Grandma and the tree fell in on the floor.

But he heard her exclaim ere she rolled out of sight,
"Merry Christmas to all and to all a GOOD NIGHT!"